Collectil

MCDONALD'S
HAPPY MEAL® TOYS

JOYCE AND TERRY LOSONSKY

4880 Lower Valley Road, Atglen, PA 19310 USA

Copyright © 1999 by Joyce and Terry Losonsky
Library of Congress Catalog Card Number: 99-63598

Designed by Bonnie M. Hensley
Type set in Cosmic Two/HumanstBT521 BT

ISBN: 0-7643-0966-8
Printed in China
1 2 3 4

Published by Schiffer Publishing Ltd.
4880 Lower Valley Road
Atglen, PA 19310
Phone: (610) 593-1777; Fax: (610) 593-2002
E-mail: Schifferbk@aol.com
Please visit our web site catalog at
www.schifferbooks.com

In Europe, Schiffer books are distributed by
Bushwood Books
6 Marksbury Avenue Kew Gardens
Surrey TW9 4JF England
Phone: 44 (0)181 392-8585;
Fax: 44 (0)181 392-9876
E-mail: Bushwd@aol.com

This book may be purchased from the publisher.
Include $3.95 for shipping. Please try your bookstore first.
We are interested in hearing from authors with book ideas on related subjects.
You may write for a free printed catalog.

Acknowledgments

Special thanks to: Mrs. Dodge and the East Middle School Team II Sixth Graders, Westminster, Maryland 21157.

Contents

Countries where McDonald's Happy Meal toys are distributed:

Number / Country / Alphabetic Abbr. / Opening Date / #Restaurants 1999

	Country	Abbr.	Opening Date	#Restaurants 1999
1.	United States	Usa	April 15, 1955	12,190
2.	Canada	Can	June 1, 1967	1,063
3.	Puerto Rico	Pue	November 10, 1967	116
4.	Virgin Islands	Vir	September 4, 1970	6
5.	Costa Rica	Cos	December 28, 1970	20
6.	Guam	Gum	June 10, 1971	6
7.	Japan	Jpn	July 20, 1971	2,640
8.	Netherlands	Net	August 21, 1971	178
9.	Panama	Pan	September 1, 1971	21
10.	Germany	Ger	November 22, 1971	878
11.	Australia	Aus	December 30, 1971	659
12.	France	Fra	June 30, 1972	680
13.	El Salvador	Sal	July 20, 1972	0
14.	Sweden	Swe	November 5, 1973	166
15.	Guatemala	Gua	June 19, 1974	24
16.	Netherland Antilles	Nea	August 16, 1974	24
17.	England	Uk	October 1, 1974	779
18.	Hong Kong	Hon	January 8, 1995	144
19.	Bahamas	Bah	August 4, 1975	3
20.	New Zealand	Zea	June 7, 1976	144
21.	Switzerland	Swi	October 20, 1976	94
22.	Ireland	Ire	May 9, 1977	40
23.	Austria	Ast	July 21, 1977	109
24.	Belgium	Bel	March 21, 1978	62
25.	Brazil	Bra	February 13, 1979	512
26.	Singapore	Sin	October 20, 1979	104
27.	Spain	Spa	March 10, 1981	163
28.	Denmark	Den	April 15, 1981	82
29.	Philippines	Phi	September 27, 1981	178
30.	Malaysia	Mal	April 29, 1982	114
31.	Norway	Nor	November 18, 1983	44
32.	Taiwan	Tai	January 28, 1984	273
33.	Andorra	And	June 29, 1984	2
34.	Wales	Wal	December 3, 1984	31
35.	Finland	Fin	December 14, 1984	85
36.	Thailand	Tha	February 23, 1985	63
37.	Aruba	Aru	April 4, 1985	2
38.	Luxembourg	Lux	July 17, 1985	4
39.	Venezuela	Ven	August 31, 1985	57
40.	Italy	Ita	October 15, 1985	183
41.	Mexico	Mex	October 29, 1985	139
42.	Cuba	Cub	April 24, 1986	1
43.	Turkey	Tur	October 24, 1986	94
44.	Argentina	Arg	November 24, 1986	148
45.	Macau	Mac	April 11, 1987	10
46.	Scotland	Sco	November 23, 1987	47
47.	Yugoslavia	Yug	March 22, 1988	14
48.	Korea	Kor	March 29, 1988	127
49.	Hungary	Hun	April 30, 1988	64
50.	Russia	Rus	January 31, 1990	39
51.	China	Chi	October 8, 1990	207
52.	Chile	Chl	November 19, 1990	30
53.	Indonesia	Ind	February 22, 1991	103
54.	Portugal	Por	May 23, 1991	50
55.	Northern Ireland	Nir	October 14, 1991	11

56. Greece	Gre	November 12, 1991	38
57. Uruguay	Uru	November 18, 1991	21
58. Martinique	Mar	December 16, 1991	5
59. Czech Republic	Cze	March 20, 1992	45
60. Guadeloupe	Gle	April 6, 1992	4
61. Poland	Pol	June 16, 1992	109
62. Monaco	Mon	November 20, 1992	1
63. Brunei	Bru	December 1, 1992	1
64. Morocco	Mor	December 18, 1992	6
65. Saipan	Sai	March 18, 1992	2
66. Iceland	Ice	September 3, 1993	2
67. Israel	Isr	October 14, 1993	57
68. Slovenia	Slo	December 4, 1993	11
69. Saudi Arabia	Sau	December 8, 1993	30
70. Oman	Oma	March 30, 1994	2
71. Kuwait	Kua	June 15, 1994	16
72. New Caledonia	Cal	July 26, 1994	1
73. Egypt	Egy	October 20, 1994	25
74. Trinidad	Tri	November 12, 1994	4
75. Bulgaria	Bul	December 10, 1994	11
76. Bahrain	Bah	December 15, 1994	5
77. Latvia	Lat	December 15, 1994	6
78. United Arab Emirates	Uar	December 21, 1994	13
79. Estonia	Est	April 29, 1995	5
80. Romania	Rom	June 16, 1995	32
81. Malta	Mal	July 7, 1995	6
82. Columbia	Col	July 14, 1995	18
83. Jamaica	Jam	September 28, 1995	9
84. Slovakia	Slv	October 13, 1995	18
85. South Africa	Saf	November 11, 1995	44
86. Jersey	Jer	December 1, 1995	1
87. Qatar	Qat	December 13, 1995	3
88. Honduras	Hon	December 14, 1995	5
89. St. Martin	Stm	December 15, 1995	1
90. Croatia	Cro	February 2, 1996	10
91. Western Samoa	Wes	March 2, 1996	1
92. Fiji	Fij	May 1, 1996	2
93. Liechtenstein	Lie	May 3, 1996	1
94. Lithuania	Lit	May 31, 1996	5
95. India	Ind	October 13, 1996	11
96. Peru	Per	October 17, 1996	7
97. Jordan	Jor	November 7, 1996	3
98. Paraguay	Par	November 21, 1996	6
99. Dominican Republic	Dor	November 30, 1996	8
100. Belarus	Bel	December 10, 1996	5
101. Tahiti	Tah	December 10, 1996	1
102. Ukraine	Ukr	May 24, 1997	10
103. Cyprus	Cyp	June 12, 1997	4
104. Macedonia	Mac	September 6, 1997	1
105. Ecudor	Ecu	October 9, 1997	4
106. Bolivia	Bol	October 24, 1997	3
107. Reunion Island	Rei	December 14, 1997	2
108. Isle of Man	Ism	December 15, 1997	1
109. Suriname	Sur	December 18, 1997	1
110. Moldova	Mol	April 30, 1998	1
111. Nicaragua	Nic	July 11, 1998	1
112. Lebanon	Leb	September 18, 1998	1
113. Pakistan	Pak	September 19, 1998	1
114. Sri Lanka	Sri	October 16, 1998	1

INTRODUCTION

A. Why Collect - For **FUN**!
   For trade with other collectors!
   For future value!

B. Where To Collect - School
   Yard sales
   Secondhand shops
   From friends
   Family toy box
   Thrift shops
   Buy them from fast food restaurants
   Relative's toy boxes!

C. When To Collect - Any time
   Free time
   Play time!

D. What To Collect - Collect toys you enjoy
   Collect clean, loose toys
   Collect new toys (MIP - mint in package)
   Collect individual toys
   Collect sets of toys!

E. What To Do With Your Collection - Play with it
   Display it on shelves in your room
   Display it at your school
   Display it at your library
   Display it at Scout meetings
   Display it at the office
   Trade with friends and family!

F. How To Keep Toys Not On Display - Store them in clean boxes
   Store them in plastic bags
   Mark your bags and boxes with toy set names!

F. Who Collects - **EVERYONE!**

G. Is There A Club For Collectors - Yes!
   Contact:
       McDonald's Collectors Club
       1153 South Lee Street, Suite 200
       Des Plaines, Illinois 60016

How to have FUN collecting?

Collectibles 101™: McDonald's® Happy Meal® Toys is designed to be a beginning book for collectors. Starting with McDonald's sets given out in 1990 and ending with current sets from 1999, this book covers Happy Meal toys from the past ten years. Collecting all these toys is easy and FUN! They are available at neighborhood yard sales and about. Organizing is also easy. Each toy is assigned a number and can be checked off as part of a set of toys. A name for the set of toys is listed at the top of the set with a number before the toy name. The numbering system represents an alphabetic label for the set and the year the set was given out, plus the number of the toy within the set. Check-off boxes are provided for marking your latest finds! One column can be used for used toys and one column for new toys. Loose, out of package, toys are more fun to enjoy, easier to arrange on shelves, easier to find, and cheaper to collect!

The range of toy prices listed is what you could expect to pay a dealer at a toy show for a toy mint in the package. Loose toys have a value of about 50% or less of the lowest value listed in the price guide. For example, a toy listed for $2.50 to $3.50 can usually be purchased at a toy show for $3.00 mint in the package or purchased for $1.00 loose. The FUN in collecting is hunting to find all these toys at yard sales, flea markets, and about for a small amount: say, $.25 or $.50 each, or less. It can be a challenge! The price range listed is not the selling price. It is the dealer price for the toy mint in package. With most dealers, these toys were acquired when the value was somewhat higher than today's value. Most dealers paid more for their stock of toys and are holding them at that higher price, because they believe the hobby will make a strong comeback. Their vision is that the kids who received the toys for free in Happy Meals will become collectors, as each toy brings back fond memories from their childhood. Most dealers will not part with a toy for less than $2.00 each, mint in the package. If you go to a show and someone is liquidating, you could get lucky and pay less for a group of toys. But, in general, the rule of thumb is: a Happy Meal toys will cost approximately $2.00 to $3.50 each to acquire at a toy show. In the end, price is determined between a buyer and the seller. Currently, there is an over supply of McDonald's Happy Meal toys on the market. Thus, the selling price is considerably less than the range listed. Dealers typically only pay 30-40% of the lowest price guide value, in the best of selling conditions. Toys should be collected for future investment, capital gain, and enjoyment. Buying them now to put away for the future is the best plan. The goal of this *Collectibles 101* series is to encourage young collectors to begin collecting and to save for future enjoyment. Along the way, "Having fun while you collect" is the golden rule!

1990

BEACH TOY HAPPY MEAL, 1990

❏ ❏   Be9001 **#1 Fry Kid Sail Boat.** Red and purple inflatable catamaran with yellow sail.
$2.00-2.50

❏ ❏   Be9002 **#2 Birdie Shovel.** Red with yellow sand propeller. $2.00-2.50

❏ ❏   Be9003 **#3 Grimace Beach Ball.** Yellow, blue, and green. $2.00-2.50

❏ ❏   Be9004 **#4 Ronald Rake Squirt Gun.** Blue and green. $2.00-2.50

❏ ❏   Be9005 **#5 Ronald Flyer Frisbee.** Inflatable turquoise and orange frisbee. $2.00-2.50

❏ ❏   Be9006 **#6 Grimace Sand Pail.** Clear plastic pail with red lid and yellow handle.
$2.00-2.50

❏ ❏   Be9007 **#7 Birdie Submarine.** Pink and blue inflatable sub. $2.00-2.50

Be9001-03

Be9004-07

Camp McDonaldland Happy Meal, 1990

❑ ❑   Cm9001 **#1 Grimace Canteen.** Blue with yellow top. 2 pieces. $2.00-2.50
❑ ❑   Cm9002 **#2 Birdie Camp Mess Kit.** Green with orange handle. 3 pieces. $2.00-2.50
❑ ❑   Cm9003 **#3 Fry Kids Knife, Fork, and Spoon.** Plastic, turquoise, or yellow fork with
         yellow or blue spoon and purple or green knife. 3 pieces. $2.00-2.50
❑ ❑   Cm9004 **#4 Ronald Collapsible Cup.** Red cup with red lid. 2 pieces. $2.50-3.50

Cm9001-04

Funny Fry Friends Happy Meal, 1990

❑ ❑   Ff9001 **#1 Hoops.** Purple kid wearing yellow sweatband holding basketball. 2 pieces.
         $4.00-5.00
❑ ❑   Ff9002 **#2 Rollin Rocker.** Yellow girl with head phones on skates. 2 pieces. $4.00-5.00
❑ ❑   Ff9003 **#3 Matey.** Red kid wearing pirate's hat. 2 pieces. $4.00-5.00
❑ ❑   Ff9004 **#4 Gadzooks.** Blue kid wearing clear glasses with bow tie. 2 pieces. $4.00-5.00

Ff9001-04

9

❑	❑	Ff9005 **#5 Tracker.** Blue kid with Safari hat and snake. 2 pieces.	$4.00-5.00
❑	❑	Ff9006 **#6 Zzz's.** Turquoise kid with sleeping cap and bear. 2 pieces.	$4.00-5.00
❑	❑	Ff9007 **#7 Too Tall.** Tall green kid with clown hat. 2 pieces.	$4.00-5.00
❑	❑	Ff9008 **#8 Sweet Cuddles.** Plum kid with baby bonnet and bottle. 2 pieces.	$4.00-5.00

Ff9005-08

JUNGLE BOOK I HAPPY MEAL, 1990

❑	❑	Ju9001 **#1 Baloo.** Gray bear.	$3.00-4.00
❑	❑	Ju9002 **#2 King Louie.** Orange orangutan.	$3.00-4.00
❑	❑	Ju9003 **#3 Kaa.** Green snake.	$3.00-4.00
❑	❑	Ju9004 **#4 Shere Khan.** Orange tiger.	$3.00-4.00

Ju9001-04

PEANUTS HAPPY MEAL, 1990

❏ ❏ Pe9001 **#1 Snoopy's Hay Hauler.** Snoopy with turquoise wagon and yellow hay. 3 pieces.
$3.50-5.00

❏ ❏ Pe9002 **#2 Charlie Brown's Tiller.** Charlie Brown with red and blue tiller and yellow sack.
3 pieces. $3.50-5.00

❏ ❏ Pe9003 **#3 Lucy's Apple Cart.** Lucy with green wheelbarrow and red apples. 3 pieces.
$3.50-5.00

❏ ❏ Pe9004 **#4 Linus Milk Mover.** Linus with orange dolly and gray milk jug with cat beside
jug. 3 pieces. $3.50-5.00

Pe9001-04

RESCUERS DOWN UNDER HAPPY MEAL, 1990

❏ ❏ Re9001 **#1 Bernard & Bianca Camera.** Green camera. $3.00-4.00
❏ ❏ Re9002 **#2 Jake Camera.** Orange Camera. $3.00-4.00
❏ ❏ Re9003 **#3 Cody Camera.** Clear Camera. $3.00-4.00
❏ ❏ Re9004 **#4 Wilbur Camera.** Purple camera. $3.00-4.00

Re9001-04

11

SUPER MARIO 3 NINTENDO HAPPY MEAL, 1990

☐ ☐ Su9001 #1 **Mario.** Spring loaded Mario pops up. $2.50-3.50
☐ ☐ Su9002 #2 **Luigi.** Luigi zooms around. $2.50-3.50
☐ ☐ Su9003 #3 **Goomba.** Goomba flips. $2.50-3.50
☐ ☐ Su9004 #4 **Koopa.** Standing Koopa hops. $2.50-3.50

Su9001-04

TALE SPIN HAPPY MEAL, 1990

☐ ☐ Ta9001 #1 **Baloo's Seaplane.** Orange and gold diecast metal airplane. $2.00-2.50
☐ ☐ Ta9002 #2 **Kit's Racing Plane.** Orange and blue diecast metal airplane. $2.00-2.50
☐ ☐ Ta9003 #3 **Molly's Biplane.** Green and red diecast metal biplane. $2.00-2.50
☐ ☐ Ta9004 #4 **Wildcat's Flying Machine.** Green and red diecast metal airplane. $2.00-2.50

Ta9001-04

1991

101 Dalmatians I Happy Meal, 1991

❏ ❏ On9101 **#1 Pogo the Dog.** Dalmatian standing. $3.00-4.00
❏ ❏ On9102 **#2 Lucky the Pup.** White and black baby dalmatian pup with red collar sitting up. $3.00-4.00
❏ ❏ On9103 **#3 Colonel and Sgt. Tibbs.** Gray sheep dog with cat on his back. $3.00-4.00
❏ ❏ On9104 **#4 Cruela Devilla.** Yellow and black villainess lady with red hands and feet. $3.00-4.00

On9101-04

MCDONALD's HAPPY MEAL TOYS ARE FUN TO COLLECT!!!

Barbie and Hot Wheels Happy Meal, 1991

Barbie Dolls:

☐ ☐ Ba9101 **#1 All American Barbie.** Barbie wearing short blue dress with Reebok sneakers. $3.00-4.00

☐ ☐ Ba9102 **#2 Costume Ball Barbie.** Barbie in pink long dress holding purple mask. $3.00-4.00

☐ ☐ Ba9103 **#3 Lights and Lace Barbie.** Barbie in pink ballerina dress on purple star shaped stand. $3.00-4.00

☐ ☐ Ba9104 **#4 Happy Birthday Barbie.** Black Barbie in long pink dress. $3.00-4.00

☐ ☐ Ba9105 **#5 Hawaiian Fun Barbie.** Hawaiian Barbie in pink beach wrap on sea shell beach stand. $3.00-4.00

☐ ☐ Ba9106 **#6 Wedding Day Midge.** Midge in white gown with pink flowers and purple ribbon. $3.00-4.00

☐ ☐ Ba9107 **#7 Ice Capades Barbie.** Barbie in purple short dress wearing white ice skates. $3.00-4.00

☐ ☐ Ba9108 **#8 My First Barbie.** Spanish Barbie in purple and white skirt with a purple top. $3.00-4.00

Ba9101-04

Ba9105-08

14

HOT WHEEL CARS:

☐	☐	Hw9101 **#1 '55 Chevy** - yellow.	$3.00-4.00
☐	☐	Hw9102 **#2 '63 Corvette** - green.	$3.00-4.00
☐	☐	Hw9103 **#3 '57 T Bird** - turquoise.	$3.00-4.00
☐	☐	Hw9104 **#4 Camaro Z-28** - purple.	$3.00-4.00
☐	☐	Hw9105 **#5 '55 Chevy** - white.	$3.00-4.00
☐	☐	Hw9106 **#6 '63 Corvette** - black.	$3.00-4.00
☐	☐	Hw9107 **#7 '57 T Bird** - red.	$3.00-4.00
☐	☐	Hw9108 **#8 Camero Z-28** - orange.	$3.00-4.00

Hw9101-04

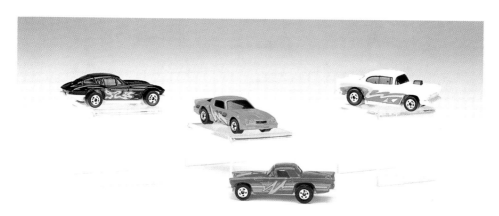

Hw9105-08

Good Morning Happy Meal, 1991

☐ ☐ Go9101 **#1 Ronald Toothbrush.** Yellow. Mint only. $2.00-3.00
☐ ☐ Go9102 **#2 Ronald Clock.** Yellow clock with Ronald's airplane propellers as hands.
                                                                $2.00-3.50
☐ ☐ Go9103 **#3 Sun Rising Cup.** Rising sun with birds and Ronald decoration plastic cup.
                                                                $2.00-2.50
☐ ☐ Go9104 **#4 Fry Kids Comb.** 5 Section Fry Kids Comb. $2.00-2.50

Go9101-04

Hook Happy Meal, 1991

☐ ☐ Ho9101 **#1 Little Mermaid Windup.** Blue Mermaid white knob windup. $3.00-4.00
☐ ☐ Ho9102 **#2 Captain Hook in Boat.** Captain Hook in blue pirate ship with orange flag.
       3 pieces. $3.00-4.00
☐ ☐ Ho9103 **#3 Rufio Squirter.** Boy floating on green rubber barrels $3.00-4.00
☐ ☐ Ho9104 **#4 Peter Pan on Purple Raft.** Yellow sail. 3 pieces. $3.00-4.00

Ho9101-04

McDino Changeables Happy Meal, 1991

❏ ❏   Mc9101 **#1 Quarter Pounder Cheese-O-Saur Changeable.** Turns into Quarter
Pounder box and turquoise dinosaur. $2.50-3.50

❏ ❏   Mc9102 **#2 McNuggets-O-Saurus Changeable.** Turns into yellow Chicken McNugget
box and green dinosaur. $2.50-3.50

❏ ❏   Mc9103 **#3 Hot Cakes-O-Dactyl Changeable.** Turns into white Hot Cakes box and
purple dinosaur. $2.50-3.50

❏ ❏   Mc9104 **#4 Big Mac-O-Saurus Rex Changeable.** Turns into Big Mac and orange dinosaur. $2.50-3.50

❏ ❏   Mc9105 **#5 Fry-Ceratops.** Turns into French Fries and yellow dinosaur. $2.50-3.50

❏ ❏   Mc9106 **#6 McDino Cone.** Turns into Ice Cream cone and blue dinosaur. $2.50-3.50

❏ ❏   Mc9107 **#7 Tri-Shake-Atops.** Turns into Shake and pink dinosaur. $2.50-3.50

❏ ❏   Mc9108 **#8 Happy Meal-O-Don.** Turns into red Happy Meal box and red dinosaur.
       $2.50-3.50

Mc9101-04

Mc9105-08

17

Nature's Helpers Happy Meal, 1991

❏ ❏	Na9101 **#1 Bird Feeder.** Green, white, and orange feeder. 3 pieces.	$2.00-2.50
❏ ❏	Na9102 **#2 Watering Can.** Blue watering can with green handle. 2 pieces.	$2.00-2.50
❏ ❏	Na9103 **#3 Terrarium.** Green base with clear dome lid. 2 pieces.	$2.00-2.50
❏ ❏	Na9104 **#4 Rake - Yellow.**	$2.00-2.50
❏ ❏	Na9105 **#5 Double Digger Trowel.** Green dirt digger. 2 pieces.	$2.00-2.50

Na9101-05

Super Looney Tunes Happy Meal, 1991

❏ ❏ Su9101 **#1 Bugs Bunny as Superbugs.** Bugs Bunny with red and blue Batman costume. 3 pieces. $2.50-3.50

❏ ❏ Su9102 **#2 Tasmanian Devil as Taz-Flash.** Taz with red devil suit. 3 pieces. $2.50-3.50

❏ ❏ Su9103 **#3 Petunia Pig as Wonder Pig.** Petunia Pig with red, white, and blue Wonder Woman suit. 3 pieces. $2.50-3.50

❏ ❏ Su9104 **#4 Daffy Duck as Bat Duck.** Daffy Duck with blue and gray Batman suit. 3 pieces. $2.50-3.50

Su9101-04

Tiny Toon Adventures Flip Cars Happy Meal, 1991

❏ ❏ Ti9101 #1 **Babs Bunny in Phone and Plucky Duck in Speed Boat.** $2.00-3.00
❏ ❏ Ti9102 #2 **Buster Bunny in Carrot and Elmira in Wagon.** $2.00-3.00
❏ ❏ Ti9103 #3 **Montana Max in Green Car and Gogo Dodo in Bath Tub.** $2.00-3.00
❏ ❏ Ti9104 #4 **Hampton Pig in Hero Sandwich and Dizzy Devil in Amp.** $2.00-3.00

Ti9101-04

1992

Back to the Future Happy Meal, 1992

❏ ❏ Bk9201 #1 **Doc's Delorean Car.** Gray and blue car with Doc hanging out the window. Sparks fly. $2.00-2.50
❏ ❏ Bk9202 #2 **Marty's Hoverboard.** Marty on pink hoverboard. $2.00-2.50
❏ ❏ Bk9203 #3 **Verne's Junkmobile.** Verne on pink, red, green, and blue wheeled vehicle. $2.00-2.50
❏ ❏ Bk9204 #4 **Einstein's Traveling Train.** Blue train with red wheels. $2.00-2.50

Bk9201-04

Barbie and Hot Wheels Mini-Streex Happy Meal, 1992

Barbie Dolls:

❏ ❏ Ba9201 **#1 Birthday Surprise Barbie.** Wearing a peach dress with brown hair.
$2.50-3.50

❏ ❏ Ba9202 **#2 My First Ballerina Barbie.** Wearing a blue dress with brown hair.
$2.50-3.50

❏ ❏ Ba9203 **#3 Rappin' Rockin Barbie.** Wearing a black shirt with yellow hair. $2.50-3.50

❏ ❏ Ba9204 **#4 Rollerblade Barbie.** Skating with pink rollerblades and yellow hair.
$2.50-3.50

❏ ❏ Ba9205 **#5 Rose Bride Barbie.** Wearing a white bride's dress. $2.50-3.50

❏ ❏ Ba9206 **#6 Snap'n Play Barbie.** Wearing a turquoise skirt and a pink and purple dress.
2 pieces. $2.50-3.50

❏ ❏ Ba9207 **#7 Sparkle Eyes Barbie.** Wearing a pink sparkle dress. $2.50-3.50

❏ ❏ Ba9208 **#8 Sun Sensation Barbie.** Wearing a gold swimsuit with turquoise wrap.
$2.50-3.50

Ba9201-08

20

Cars With Launchers:

❏ ❏   Sx9201 **#1 Black Arrow Car.** Black, purple, and green car with pink launcher.
$2.00-2.50

❏ ❏   Sx9202 **#2 Blade Burner Car.** Yellow, blue, and pink car with light blue launcher.
$2.00-2.50

❏ ❏   Sx9203 **#3 Flame-Out Car.** Blue, red, and yellow car with red launcher. $2.00-2.50

❏ ❏   Sx9204 **#4 Hot Shock Car.** Red, purple, and yellow car with yellow launcher.
$2.00-2.50

❏ ❏   Sx9205 **#5 Night Shadow Car.** Black, blue, green, yellow, and pink car with purple, pinkish launcher. $2.00-2.50

❏ ❏   Sx9206 **#6 Quick-Flash Car.** Purple, blue, and green car with purple launcher.
$2.00-2.50

❏ ❏   Sx9207 **#7 Racer-Tracer Car.** Green, pink, and blue car with green launcher
$2.00-2.50

❏ ❏   Sx9208 **#8 Turbo Flyer Car.** Blue, yellow, and pink car with dark blue launcher.
$2.00-2.50

Sx9201-04

Sx9205-08

21

Batman Happy Meal, 1992

❏ ❏   Bt9201 **#1 Batman Batmissle.** Black car with Batman inside. $3.00-3.50

❏ ❏   Bt9202 **#2 Batmobile.** Black Batmissile inside a Batmobile. 2 pieces. $3.00-3.50

❏ ❏   Bt9203 **#3 Catwoman Cat Coupe.** Purple Catwoman mobile with Batwoman inside. $3.00-3.50

❏ ❏   Bt9204 **#4 Penguin Roto-Roadster.** Yellow car with Penguin inside. $3.00-3.50

Bt9201-04

Behind the Scenes Happy Meal, 1992

❏ ❏   Be9201 **#1 Animation Wheel.** Black and blue circle can with cartoon strips. 2 pieces. $2.00-2.50

❏ ❏   Be9202 **#2 Balance Builders.** Orange, blue, yellow, green, and red stacking figures. 5 pieces. $2.00-2.50

❏ ❏   Be9203 **#3 Rub and Draw Templates.** 6 Templates with a turquoise holder. 7 pieces. $2.00-2.50

❏ ❏   Be9204 **#4 Rainbow Viewer.** Turquoise and purple viewer. $2.00-2.50

Be9201-04

CABBAGE PATCH KIDS AND TONKA TRUCKS HAPPY MEAL, 1992

CABBAGE PATCH DOLLS:

❑ ❑   Cp9201 **#1 All Dressed Up CPK.** CPK dressed in a red party dress, holding a gift.
$2.00-2.50

❑ ❑   Cp9202 **#2 Tiny Dancer CPK.** CPK dressed as a tiny ballerina in a purple body suit.
$2.00-2.50

❑ ❑   Cp9203 **#3 Fun on Ice CPK.** CPK dressed in a green and red dress with a white muff, wearing ice skates.
$2.00-2.50

❑ ❑   Cp9204 **#4 Holiday Dreamer CPK.** Dressed in pink and blue pajamas with a green stocking and bear.
$2.00-2.50

❑ ❑   Cp9205 **#5 Holiday Pageant CPK.** Dressed as a white angel with long golden hair.
$2.00-2.50

Cp9201-05

TONKA TRUCKS:

❑ ❑	Tk9201 **#1 Loader Vehicle** - yellow.	$2.00-2.50
❑ ❑	Tk9202 **#2 Cement Mixer** - orange.	$2.00-2.50
❑ ❑	Tk9203 **#3 Dump Truck** - yellow.	$2.00-2.50
❑ ❑	Tk9204 **#4 Fire Truck** - red.	$2.00-2.50
❑ ❑	Tk9205 **#5 Backhoe Vehicle** - blue.	$2.00-2.50

Tk9201-05

Michael Jordan Fitness Fun Happy Meal, 1992

☐ ☐　Mj9201 **#1 Baseball.** White with MJ logo.　$4.00-5.00
☐ ☐　Mj9202 **#2 Basketball.** Orange with MJ logo.　$4.00-5.00
☐ ☐　Mj9203 **#3 Flying Disc Frisbee.** Turquoise with MJ logo.　$4.00-5.00
☐ ☐　Mj9204 **#4 Football.** Green and turquoise with MJ logo.　$4.00-5.00
☐ ☐　Mj9205 **#5 Jump Rope.** Green with purple handles.　$4.00-5.00
☐ ☐　Mj9206 **#6 Soccer Ball.** Inflatable black and white soccer ball with MJ logo.　$4.00-4.00
☐ ☐　Mj9207 **#7 Stop Watch.** Yellow dial stop watch with MJ logo.　$4.00-5.00
☐ ☐　Mj9208 **#8 Water Bottle.** Blue water bottle with purple lid and orange straw with MJ logo.
$4.00-5.00

Mj9201-04

Mj9205-08

24

MYSTERY OF THE LOST ARCHES HAPPY MEAL, 1992

❏ ❏   My9201 **#1 Magic Lens Camera.** Plastic blue camera. $2.00-2.50
❏ ❏   My9202 **#2 Micro-Cassette Magnifier.** Green cassette with magnifier. $2.00-2.50
❏ ❏   My9203 **#3 Phone as a Periscope.** Orange phone twists into a periscope. $2.00-2.50
❏ ❏   My9204 **#4 Flashlight and Telescope.** Red and blue or red and yellow telescope.
     $2.00-2.50

My9201-04

NATURE'S WATCH HAPPY MEAL, 1992

❏ ❏   Na9201 **#1 Bird Feeder.** Orange lid with clear container and yellow bottom. 3 pieces.
     $2.00-2.50
❏ ❏   Na9202 **#2 Double Shovel and Rake.** Red shovel and purple rake. 2 pieces.
     $2.00-2.50
❏ ❏   Na9203 **#3 Greenhouse.** Clear dome top with green bottom. 2 pieces. $2.00-2.50
❏ ❏   Na9204 **#4 Sprinkler as Watering Can.** Green watering can with yellow nozzle.
     $2.00-2.50

Na9201-04

Tiny Toon Adventures Happy Meal, 1992

❏	❏	Ti9201 **#1 Babs Bunny with Record Player.** Pink Bunny with Tiny Toons record player in bubble. $2.00-2.50
❏	❏	Ti9202 **#2 Buster Bunny in Bumper Car.** Blue Bunny in red bumper car and basketball in bubble. $2.00-2.50
❏	❏	Ti9203 **#3 Dizzy Devil in Car.** Purple Dizzy Devil in orange bubble car with spinner in bubble. $2.00-2.50
❏	❏	Ti9204 **#4 Elmyra in Green Car.** Girl with yellow hat in green car with bunny in bubble. $2.00-2.50
❏	❏	Ti9205 **#5 Gogo Dodo in Rolling Car.** Green Gogo Dodo on yellow three wheel roller with front wheel as bubble. $2.00-2.50
❏	❏	Ti9206 **#6 Montana Max in Cash Register Car.** Max in green car and cash register as bubble. $2.00-2.50
❏	❏	Ti9207 **#7 Plucky Duck in Steam Roller.** Plucky Duck in blue steam roller car with bubble back wheel. $2.00-2.50
❏	❏	Ti9208 **#8 Sweetie on Pavement Roller.** Pink bunny on pavement roller with front wheel as bubble. $2.00-2.50

Above: Ti9201-04

Below: Ti9205-08

Young Astronauts Happy Meal, 1992

❑ ❑	As9201 **#1 Command Module.** Cardboard. 13 pieces.	$2.00-2.50
❑ ❑	As9202 **#2 Lunar Rover.** Cardboard. 13 pieces.	$2.00-2.50
❑ ❑	As9203 **#3 Satellite Dish.** Cardboard. 8 pieces.	$2.00-2.50
❑ ❑	As9204 **#4 Space Shuttle.** Cardboard. 10 pieces.	$2.00-2.50

As9201-04

McDonald's Happy Meal toys are FUN to SHARE with Friends and Family!

27

1993

BARBIE AND HOT WHEELS HAPPY MEAL, 1993

BARBIE DOLLS:

❏ ❏   Ba9301 **#1 Birthday Party Barbie.** Black Barbie holding a birthday cake. $2.00-2.50

❏ ❏   Ba9302 **#2 Hollywood Hair Barbie.** Barbie in a gold short dress on a blue star base.
  $2.00-2.50

❏ ❏   Ba9303 **#3 My First Ballerina Barbie.** Barbie in a purple ballerina dress with brown long hair. $2.00-2.50

❏ ❏   Ba9304 **#4 Paint 'N Dazzle Barbie.** Barbie in a pink short skirt on a "B" stage with long yellow hair. $2.00-2.50

❏ ❏   Ba9305 **#5 Romantic Bride Barbie.** Barbie in a white long gown with a peach bouquet and long yellow hair. $2.00-2.50

❏ ❏   Ba9306 **#6 Secret Heart Barbie.** Barbie in a white and rose long gown holding a red heart with long yellow hair. $2.00-2.50

❏ ❏   Ba9307 **#7 Twinkle Lights Barbie.** Barbie in a pink and white gown with a white purse and long yellow hair. $2.00-2.50

❏ ❏   Ba9308 **#8 Western Stampin' Barbie.** Barbie in a blue and silver western outfit with a cowgirl hat. $2.00-2.50

Ba9301-04

Ba9305-08

Hot Wheel Cars:

❏ ❏ Hw9301 **#1 McDonald's Funny Car.** Red and white car with "McDonald's" on side.
$3.00-3.50

❏ ❏ Hw9302 **#2 Quaker State Racer #62 Car.** Green Quaker State #62 car. $3.00-3.50

❏ ❏ Hw9303 **#3 McDonald's Thunderbird #27 Car.** Red Thunderbird #27 with "M" logo on hood. $3.00-3.50

❏ ❏ Hw9304 **#4 Hot Wheels Funny Car.** White, red, and yellow car with "Hot Wheels" on side of Funny Car. $3.00-3.50

❏ ❏ Hw9305 **#5 McDonald's Dragster Car.** Red Dragster car with "McDonald's" logo on side and hood. $3.00-3.50

❏ ❏ Hw9306 **#6 Hot Wheels Camaro #1 Car.** Blue Camaro with "Hot Wheels 1" on side.
$3.00-3.50

❏ ❏ Hw9307 **#7 Duracell Racer #88 Car.** Yellow car with "Duracell" on side and hood.
$3.00-3.50

❏ ❏ Hw9308 **#8 Hot Wheels Dragster Car.** Black and yellow Dragster car with "Hot Wheels" on side. $3.00-3.50

Hw9301-04

Hw9305-08

29

❏ ❏ Bt9301 **#1 Joker in a Car.** Purple car with yellow wheels. $3.00-3.50

❏ ❏ Bt9302 **#2 Poison Ivy in a Car.** Red headed woman in a green car. $3.00-3.50

❏ ❏ Bt9303 **#3 Robin on a Motorcycle.** Robin on a red motorcycle with a large "R" on the front. $3.00-3.50

❏ ❏ Bt9304 **#4 Two Face in a Car.** White and black two face in a white flip style car with red wheels. $3.00-3.50

❏ ❏ Bt9305 **#5 Batgirl.** Gray Batgirl with blue cape. $3.00-3.50

❏ ❏ Bt9306 **#6 Batman.** Gray and black Batman with black removable cape. 2 pieces. $3.00-3.50

❏ ❏ Bt9307 **#7 Catwoman with a Leopard.** Gray and black Catwoman with a yellow leopard. 2 pieces. $3.00-3.50

❏ ❏ Bt9308 **#8 Riddler.** Figurine wearing a green jacket, gray tie, and purple mask. $3.00-3.50

Bt9301-04

Bt9305-08

DINO - MOTION DINOSAURS HAPPY MEAL, 1993

❏ ❏ Di9301 **#1 Baby Sinclair.** Yellow baby dinosaur holding a pot with a green push gear.
$2.00-2.50

❏ ❏ Di9302 **#2 Charlene Sinclair.** Wearing a purple blouse holding a phone with orange push gear.
$2.00-2.50

❏ ❏ Di9303 **#3 Earl Sinclair.** Blue and green father holding a lunch box with a yellow push gear.
$2.00-2.50

❏ ❏ Di9304 **#4 Fran Sinclair.** Wearing pink apron mother holding a spoon with a purple push gear.
$2.00-2.50

❏ ❏ Di9305 **#5 Grandma Ethyl.** Wearing a pink dress sitting in a chair with a pink push gear.
$2.00-2.50

❏ ❏ Di9306 **#6 Robbie Sinclair.** Wearing a red shirt holding a guitar with a turquoise push gear.
$2.00-2.50

Di9301-06

FIELD TRIP HAPPY MEAL, 1993

❏ ❏ Fi9301 **#1 Nature Viewer.** Magnifier collection tube. 2 pieces. $2.00-2.50
❏ ❏ Fi9302 **#2 Leaf Printer.** Yellow leaf holder. $2.00-2.50
❏ ❏ Fi9303 **#3 Kaleidoscope.** Red and blue specimen viewer. $2.00-2.50
❏ ❏ Fi9304 **#4 Vinyl Collection Bag.** White and green plastic collection bag marked "Field Trip." $2.00-2.50

Fi9301-04

Food Fundamentals Happy Meal, 1993

☐ ☐ Fo9301 **#1 Milly Milk Carton.** White plastic milk carton with arms. $2.00-2.50
☐ ☐ Fo9302 **#2 Otis Sandwich with Helmet.** Sandwich shaped figure with arms and a blue helmet. $2.00-2.50
☐ ☐ Fo9303 **#3 Ruby Red Apple.** Red apple shaped figure with yellow arms. $2.00-2.50
☐ ☐ Fo9304 **#4 Slugger with Baseball Hat.** Steak shaped figure with blue arms and green baseball cap. $2.00-2.50

Fo9301-04

Halloween McNugget Buddies Happy Meal, 1993

☐ ☐ Ha9301 **#1 McBoo McNugget.** White ghost with McNugget body. 2 pieces. $3.00-3.50
☐ ☐ Ha9302 **#2 Monster McNugget.** Wearing a green hat, purple pants, and green hands. 3 pieces. $3.00-3.50
☐ ☐ Ha9303 **#3 Mummy McNugget.** Wrapped in white bandages with a spider on its head. 3 pieces. $3.00-3.50
☐ ☐ Ha9304 **#4 McNuggla.** Wearing a black hat, black cape, and a bat on its head. 3 pieces. $3.00-3.50
☐ ☐ Ha9305 **#5 Pumpkin McNugget.** Orange pumpkin hat / pumpkin base. 3 pieces. $3.00-3.50
☐ ☐ Ha9306 **#6 Witchie McNugget.** Wearing a black witch's hat with a purple cape and broom. 3 pieces. $3.00-3.50

Ha9301-03

Ha9304-06

Looney Tunes Quack Up Car Chase Happy Meal, 1993

- ❑ ❑   Lo9301 **#1 Bugs Super Stretch Limo.** Bugs Bunny in a red or orange stretch limousine.
$2.00-2.50
- ❑ ❑   Lo9302 **#2 Daffy Splittin Sports Car.** Daffy Duck in a yellow split apart car.
$2.00-2.50
- ❑ ❑   Lo9303 **#3 Porky Ghost Catcher Truck.** Porky Pig in a green truck with a ghost popping out of the top.
$2.00-2.50
- ❑ ❑   Lo9304 **#4 Taz Tornado Tracker Jeep.** Taz in a turquoise jeep.
$2.00-2.50

Lo9301-04

33

M Squad Happy Meal, 1993

☐ ☐   Ms9301 **#1 Spy-Coder Walkie Talkie.** Orange and black walkie-talkie with red decoder
           shield. 3 pieces. $2.00-2.50

☐ ☐   Ms9302 **#2 Spy-Noculars Binoculars.** Red and blue video cam that turns into binoculars.
                                                                   $2.00-2.50

☐ ☐   Ms9303 **#3 Spy-Stamper Pad Calculator.** Yellow calculator with ink pad stamper. 2 pieces.
                                                                   $2.00-2.50

☐ ☐   Ms9304 **#4 Spy-Tracker Watch.** Watch becomes a compass. $2.00-2.50

Ms9301-04

Nickelodeon Game Gadgets Happy Meal, 1993

☐ ☐   Ni9301 **#1 Applause Paws.** Yellow clapping hands on a blue base. $2.00-2.50
☐ ☐   Ni9302 **#2 Blimp Shaped Game.** Green blimp with spin game. $2.00-2.50
☐ ☐   Ni9303 **#3 Gotcha Gusher.** Green and pink fly spray can squirter. $2.00-2.50
☐ ☐   Ni9304 **#4 Loud-Mouth Mike.** Pink and green microphone. $2.00-2.50

Ni9301-04

Out for Fun Happy Meal, 1993

❏ ❏   Ou9301 **#1 Beach Ball.** Blue beach ball showing Ronald in a hot air balloon. $2.00-2.50
❏ ❏   Ou9302 **#2 Bubble Making Shoe.** Red shoe with a yellow tray. Ronald's shoe changes
     to bubble maker. 2 pieces. $2.00-2.50
❏ ❏   Ou9303 **#3 Sand Pail.** White pail with yellow handle, shows Ronald and friends at beach.
                                                              $2.00-2.50
❏ ❏   Ou9304 **#4 Sunglasses.** Blue and green sunglasses. $2.00-2.50

Ou9301-04

Snow White and the Seven Dwarfs Happy Meal, 1993

❏ ❏   Sn9301 **#1 Bashful.** Bashful peeks up from brown diamond mine cart. $2.50-3.50
❏ ❏   Sn9302 **#2 Doc.** Doc pushing cart full of diamonds. $2.50-3.50
❏ ❏   Sn9303 **#3 Dopey on top of Sneezy.** Dopey on top of Sneezy in blue long coat.
                                                             $2.50-3.50
❏ ❏   Sn9304 **#4 Happy and Grumpy.** Happy and Grumpy on railroad push cart. $2.50-3.50

Sn9301-04

❑ ❑ Sn9305 **#5 Prince on Horse.** Prince with red cape riding white horse. $3.00-5.00
❑ ❑ Sn9306 **#6 Queen as the Witch.** Queen with black dress changes to witch. 2 pieces.
$3.00-5.00
❑ ❑ Sn9307 **#7 Sleepy.** Sleepy with white long beard has arms raised to open eyes.
$2.50-3.50
❑ ❑ Sn9308 **#8 Snow White with Wishing Well.** Snow White in yellow dress next to green
wishing well. 2 pieces. $2.50-3.50

Sn9305-08

Totally Toy Holiday Happy Meal, 1993

☐ ☐ To9301 **#1 Sally Secrets Doll.** Black or white doll with pink dress. $2.00-2.50

☐ ☐ To9302 **#2 Lil Miss Candi Stripes.** Girl with yellow hair has red and white dress which snaps onto green. 2 pieces. $2.00-2.50

☐ ☐ To9303 **#3 Magic Nursery Doll.** Blue pajama stuffed doll with plastic face. $2.00-2.50

☐ ☐ To9304 **#4 Polly Pocket.** Green/red hinged case with yellow figure. $2.00-2.50

☐ ☐ To9305 **#5 Key Force Truck.** Black and red truck with purple key on roof. $2.00-2.50

☐ ☐ To9306 **#6 Attack Pack Vehicle.** Blue shark-like car with hook. $2.00-2.50

☐ ☐ To9307 **#7 Key Force Car.** Red car with gray key on roof. $2.00-2.50

☐ ☐ To9308 **#8 Mighty Max.** White skull-shaped Mighty Max with attached yellow figure. $2.00-2.50

☐ ☐ To9309 **#9 Tattoo Car.** Green car with crocodile decals. $2.00-2.50

To9301-04

To9305-09

37

1994

ANIMANIACS HAPPY MEAL, 1994

❏ ❏   An9401 **#1 Bicycle Built for Trio.** 3 figures riding a purple bike. $2.00-2.50

❏ ❏   An9402 **#2 Dot's Ice Cream Machine.** Ice cream truck with pink wheels and Dot pushing. $2.00-2.50

❏ ❏   An9403 **#3 Goodskate Goodfeathers.** 3 bird-like characters on a yellow skateboard. $2.00-2.50

❏ ❏   An9404 **#4 Mindy and Buttons on Vehicle.** Two characters riding turquoise vehicle. $2.00-2.50

❏ ❏   An9405 **#5 Pinky on the Brain Mobile.** White figure on orange tricycle. $2.00-2.50

❏ ❏   An9406 **#6 Slappy and Skippy in Sidecar.** A figure in the pink car and one in the green side car. $2.00-2.50

❏ ❏   An9407 **#7 Wakko Upside-Down Vehicle.** Upside-down figure on green tricycle. $2.00-2.50

❏ ❏   An9408 **#8 Yakko Riding on Heavy Ralph.** Figure riding heavy man on tricycle. $2.00-2.50

An9401-04

An9405-08

Barbie and Hot Wheels Happy Meal, 1994

Barbie Dolls:

❑ ❑ Ba9401 **#1 Bicycling Barbie.** Barbie in green outfit on pink bike. $2.00-2.50

❑ ❑ Ba9402 **#2 Jewel/Glitter Shani Barbie.** Black Barbie with orange dress and long black hair. $2.00-2.50

❑ ❑ Ba9403 **#3 Camp Barbie.** Barbie wearing pink jacket, tee shirt, and blue shorts on green base. $2.00-2.50

❑ ❑ Ba9404 **#4 Camp Teresa Barbie.** Barbie in blue shirt and yellow pants. $2.00-2.50

❑ ❑ Ba9405 **#5 Locket Surprise Barbie.** White or black Barbie in pink party dress on gold stand. $2.00-2.50

❑ ❑ Ba9406 **#6 Locket Surprise Ken.** White or black Ken with gold jacket and turquoise pants. $2.00-2.50

❑ ❑ Ba9407 **#7 Jewel and Glitter Bride.** Barbie in long wedding dress holding pink flowers. $2.00-2.50

❑ ❑ Ba9408 **#8 Bridesmaid Skipper.** Skipper in light purple dress with light yellow hair. $2.00-2.50

Ba9401-04

Ba9405-08

39

Hot Wheel Cars:

☐ ☐ Hw9409 **#9 Bold Eagle** - yellow and silver Hot Rod. $2.00-2.50

☐ ☐ Hw9410 **#10 Black Cat** - black Hot Rod. $2.00-2.50

☐ ☐ Hw9411 **#11 Flame Rider** - black Hot Rod with red flame decal. $2.00-2.50

☐ ☐ Hw9412 **#12 Gas Hog** - red convertible. $2.00-2.50

☐ ☐ Hw9413 **#13 Turbine 4-2** - blue sleek car. $2.00-2.50

☐ ☐ Hw9414 **#14 2-Cool** - purple and silver sports car. $2.00-2.50

☐ ☐ Hw9415 **#15 Street Shocker** - green sports car. $2.00-2.50

☐ ☐ Hw9416 **#16 X21J Cruiser** - blue and silver Formula I car. $2.00-2.50

Hw9409-12

Hw9413-16

Bobby's World Happy Meal, 1994

❏ ❏   Bo9401 **#1 Bobby on a 3-Wheeler inside a Bumper Car.** Bobby on yellow three-wheeler with red bumper car. 3 pieces. $2.00-2.50

❏ ❏   Bo9402 **#2 Bobby on an Innertube inside a Bumper Car.** Bobby on a green innertube inside an orange bumper car. 2 pieces $2.00-2.50

❏ ❏   Bo9403 **#3 Bobby on Skates inside a Bumper Car.** Bobby on a blue skateboard inside a green bumper car. 3 pieces. $2.00-2.50

❏ ❏   Bo9404 **#4 Bobby in a Wagon inside a Bumper Car.** Bobby in a red wagon inside a blue bumper car. 3 pieces. $2.00-2.50

Bo9401-04

Cabbage Patch Kids and Tonka Trucks Happy Meal, 1994

Cabbage Patch Kids:

❏ ❏   Cp9401 **#1 Mimi Kristina CPK.** CPK with a purple and white long dress as an Angel with a gold horn. $2.00-2.50

❏ ❏   Cp9402 **#2 Kimberly Katherine CPK.** CPK in a red and green dress as Santa's helper with reddish yarn hair. $2.00-2.50

❏ ❏   Cp9403 **#3 Abigail Lynn CPK.** Black CPK doll in a red toy soldier outfit with a blue top hat, holding a candy cane. $2.00-2.50

❏ ❏   Cp9404 **#4 Michelle Elyse CPK.** CPK dressed as a snow fairy in a long white dress holding a snowflake. $2.00-2.50

Cp9401-04

Tonka Trucks:

☐ ☐   Tk9405 **#5 Loader** - orange and black lift. $2.00-2.50
☐ ☐   Tk9406 **#6 Crane** - green with black hook. $2.00-2.50
☐ ☐   Tk9407 **#7 Grader** - yellow with yellow blade. $2.00-2.50
☐ ☐   Tk9408 **#8 Bulldozer** - yellow with black blade. $2.00-2.50

Tk9405-08

Earth Days Happy Meal, 1994

☐ ☐   Ea9401 **#1 Binoculars.** Green with eye pieces shaped like the globe. $2.00-2.50
☐ ☐   Ea9402 **#2 Bird feeder.** Bird house shaped with a green roof. $2.00-2.50
☐ ☐   Ea9403 **#3 Terrarium as a Globe.** Clear cylinder top with blue bottom. $2.00-2.50
☐ ☐   Ea9404 **#4 Tool Carrier.** Blue rectangle plastic box with a red shovel and yellow carry strap. 3 pieces. $2.00-2.50

Ea9401-04

FLINTSTONES HAPPY MEAL, 1994

❑ ❑   FI9401 **#1 Barney's Fossil Fill-Up House.** Gray building with Barney in a car. 3 pieces.
$1.50-2.50

❑ ❑   FI9402 **#2 Betty, Bamm Bamm, and Roc Donald's House.** Yellow building and Betty in a brown log car. 3 pieces.
$1.50-2.50

❑ ❑   FI9403 **#3 Fred's Bedrock Bowl-O-Rama House.** Green building with Fred in a red car. 3 pieces.
$1.50-2.50

❑ ❑   FI9404 **#4 Pebbles and Dino's Toys-S-A House.** Red building with Peebbles on a blue cycle. 3 pieces.
$1.50-2.50

❑ ❑   FI9405 **#5 Wilma Flinstone's House.** Peach building with Wilma in gray car. 3 pieces.
$1.50-2.50

FI9401-05

43

Happy Birthday Train Happy Meal, 1994

❏	❏	Fi9401 #1 Ronald McDonald in red Happy Meal box.	$2.00-3.00
❏	❏	Fi9402 #2 Barbie as Ballerina.	$3.00-4.00
❏	❏	Fi9403 #3 Hot Wheels Racing.	$2.00-3.00
❏	❏	Fi9404 #4 E.T. on Stage.	$2.00-3.00
❏	❏	Fi9405 #5 Sonic the Hedgehog on TV.	$2.00-3.00
❏	❏	Fi9406 #6 Berenstain Bears on See Saw.	$2.00-3.00
❏	❏	Fi9407 #7 Cabbage Patch Kids on Rocking Horse.	$2.00-3.00
❏	❏	Fi9408 #8 Tonka Truck Carrying a Red Package.	$8.00-10.00
❏	❏	Fi9409 #9 101 Dalmatians on Box.	$3.00-4.00
❏	❏	Fi9410 #10 Peanuts on Calliope.	$3.00-4.00
❏	❏	Fi9411 #11 Miss Piggy and Kermit Dancing.	$2.00-3.00
❏	❏	Fi9412 #12 Little Mermaid with Flounder.	$2.00-3.00
❏	❏	Fi9413 #13 Tiny Toons Rabbits.	$2.00-3.00
❏	❏	Fi9414 #14 Bugs Bunny Playing Symbols.	$3.00-4.00
❏	❏	Fi9415 #15 Happy Meal Guys Blowing Party Horn.	$2.00-3.00

Fi9401

Fi9401-04

Fi9405-08

Fi9409-12

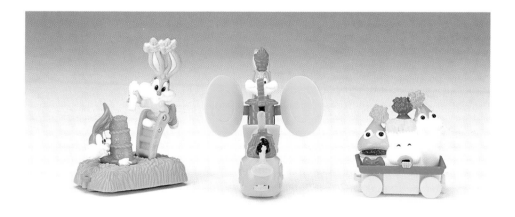

Fi9413-15

45

MAGIC SCHOOL BUS HAPPY MEAL, 1994

❏ ❏ Ma9401 **#1 Collector Card Kit.** Yellow school bus with ten collector cards.
$2.00-2.50

❏ ❏ Ma9402 **#2 Geo Fossil Finder.** Stacking fossil layer tracing stencil. 4 pieces. $2.00-2.50
❏ ❏ Ma9403 **#3 Space Tracer.** Blue tracing protractor showing the planets. $2.00-2.50
❏ ❏ Ma9404 **#4 Undersea Adventure Game.** Green bead game with yellow clip.
$2.00-2.50

Ma9401-04

MAKING MOVIES HAPPY MEAL, 1994

❏ ❏ Mm9401 **#1 Clapboard.** Black chalk board. $2.00-2.50
❏ ❏ Mm9402 **#2 Megaphone.** Red and yellow megaphone. $2.00-2.50
❏ ❏ Mm9403 **#3 Movie Camera.** Blue movie camera with a black crank. $2.00-2.50
❏ ❏ Mm9404 **#4 Sound Effects Machine.** Purple sound rectangle machine. $2.00-2.50

Mm9401-04

46

MICKEY & FRIENDS HAPPY MEAL, 1994

❏ ❏	Mi9401 **#1 Chip in China** - wearing a Chinese hat.		$2.00-2.50
❏ ❏	Mi9402 **#2 Daisy in Germany** - with purple dress.		$2.00-2.50
❏ ❏	Mi9403 **#3 Dale in Morocco** - with purple vest and hat with tassel.		$2.00-2.50
❏ ❏	Mi9404 **#4 Donald in Mexico** - with large orange sombrero hat.		$2.00-2.50
❏ ❏	Mi9405 **#5 Goofy in Norway** - with blue hat.		$2.00-2.50
❏ ❏	Mi9406 **#6 Mickey in USA** - red tall hat.		$2.00-2.50
❏ ❏	Mi9407 **#7 Minnie in Japan** - with blue Japanese dress.		$2.00-2.50
❏ ❏	Mi9408 **#8 Pluto in France** - with blue French hat.		$2.00-2.50

Mi9401-04

Mi9405-08

Sonic 3 the Hedgehog Happy Meal, 1994

☐	☐	So9401 **#1 Dr. Ivo Robotnik** - in gray auto.	$2.00-2.50
☐	☐	So9402 **#2 Knuckles** - red figure in white cloud.	$2.00-2.50
☐	☐	So9403 **#3 Sonic the Hedgehog** - on orange base. 2 pieces.	$2.00-2.50

So9401-03

1995

Amazing Wildlife Happy Meal, 1995

☐	☐	Am9501 **#1 Asiatic Lion** - stuffed.	$2.00-2.50
☐	☐	Am9502 **#2 Chimpanzee** - stuffed.	$2.00-2.50
☐	☐	Am9503 **#3 African Elephant** - stuffed.	$2.00-2.50
☐	☐	Am9504 **#4 Koala** - stuffed.	$2.00-2.50
☐	☐	Am9505 **#5 Dromedary Camel** - stuffed.	$2.00-2.50
☐	☐	Am9506 **#6 Galapagos Tortoise** - stuffed.	$2.00-2.50
☐	☐	Am9507 **#7 Polar Bear** - stuffed.	$2.00-2.50
☐	☐	Am9508 **#8 Siberian Tiger** - stuffed.	$2.00-2.50

Am9501-04

Am9505-08

Animaniacs Happy Meal, 1995

❏ ❏	An9501 **#1 Pinky & the Brain** - in pink vehicle lifting a blue ball.	$2.00-2.50
❏ ❏	An9502 **#2 Goodfeathers** - in red truck with yellow key.	$2.00-2.50
❏ ❏	An9503 **#3 Dot and Ralph** - in blue and red vehicle.	$2.00-2.50
❏ ❏	An9504 **#4 Wakko and Yakko** - in blue launcher vehicle.	$2.00-2.50
❏ ❏	An9505 **#5 Slappy and Skippy** - in yellow helicopter.	$2.00-2.50
❏ ❏	An9506 **#6 Mindy and Buttons** - in blue baby carriage.	$2.00-2.50
❏ ❏	An9507 **#7 Wakko, Yakko, and Dot** - in red and yellow rocket.	$2.00-2.50
❏ ❏	An9508 **#8 Hip Hippos** - in purplish, pink boat.	$2.00-2.50

An9501-04

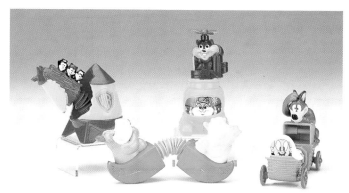

An9505-08

49

Barbie and Hot Wheels Happy Meal, 1995

Barbie Dolls:

❏ ❏ Ba9501 **#1 Hot Skating Barbie.** Barbie in turquoise and pink outfit with yellow skates.
$2.00-2.50

❏ ❏ Ba9502 **#2 Dance Moves Barbie.** Barbie in pink and yellow tutu with yellow dancing shoes on green stand. 2 pieces. $2.00-2.50

❏ ❏ Ba9503 **#3 Butterfly Princess Teresa.** Barbie in pink long dress with cutouts holding yellow butterfly. $2.00-2.50

❏ ❏ Ba9504 **#4 Cool Country Barbie.** Barbie in purple and pink cow girl outfit riding a beige horse. $2.00-2.50

❏ ❏ Ba9505 **#5 Lifeguard Ken.** Black or white Ken with yellow jet ski. 2 pieces. $2.00-2.50

❏ ❏ Ba9506 **#6 Lifeguard Barbie.** Black or white Barbie in red, white, and blue outfit holding binoculars. $2.00-2.50

❏ ❏ Ba9507 **#7 Bubble Angel Barbie.** Barbie in blue wrap with butterfly wings. 2 pieces.
$2.00-2.50

❏ ❏ Ba9508 **#8 Ice Skatin' Barbie.** Black Barbie with turquoise outfit skating on blue stand. 2 pieces. $2.00-2.50

Ba9501-04

Ba9505-08

Hot Wheels Cars:

◻ ◻ Hw9509 **#9 Lightning Speed** - orange and blue car with clear dome. $2.00-2.50
◻ ◻ Hw9510 **#10 Shock Force** - black Hot Rod with silver pipes. $2.00-2.50
◻ ◻ Hw9511 **#11 Twin Engine** - green car with silver engine. $2.00-2.50
◻ ◻ Hw9512 **#12 Radar Racer** - blue car with clear dome top. $2.00-2.50
◻ ◻ Hw9513 **#13 Blue Bandit** - blue car with black raised hood. $2.00-2.50
◻ ◻ Hw9514 **#14 Power Circuit** - red car with yellow accents. $2.00-2.50
◻ ◻ Hw9515 **#15 Black Burner** - red car with silver accents. $2.00-2.50
◻ ◻ Hw9516 **#16 After Blast** - yellow car with black accents. $2.00-2.50

Hw9509-12

Hw9513-16

THE BUSY WORLD OF RICHARD SCARRY HAPPY MEAL, 1995

❏ ❏   Ri9501 **#1 Lowly Worm Red Apple Vehicle and Blue Post Office.** Red apple with blue post office made of cardboard. 3 pieces $2.00-2.50

❏ ❏   Ri9502 **#2 Huckle Cat in Blue Vehicle and Yellow School.** Cat in blue car with yellow school made of cardboard. 3 pieces. $2.00-2.50

❏ ❏   Ri9503 **#3 Mr. Frumble in Green Vehicle and Red Fire Station.** Mr. Frumble in yellow car with red fire station made of cardboard. 3 pieces. $2.00-2.50

❏ ❏   Ri9504 **#4 Banana Gorilla in Yellow Vehicle and Green Grocery Store.** Banana Gorilla in yellow car with green grocery store made of cardboard. 3 pieces. $2.00-2.50

Ri9501-04

DISNEYLAND 40 YEARS OF ADVENTURE HAPPY MEAL, 1995

❏ ❏   Di9501 **#1 Brer Bear** - in log boat. $2.00-2.50
❏ ❏   Di9502 **#2 Aladdin & Jasmine** - on elephant. $2.00-2.50
❏ ❏   Di9503 **#3 Simba** - on Rock Mountain. $2.00-2.50
❏ ❏   Di9504 **#4 Mickey Mouse** - in red space car. $2.00-2.50
❏ ❏   Di9505 **#5 Roger Rabbit** - in yellow car. $2.00-2.50
❏ ❏   Di9506 **#6 Winnie Pooh** - in red train. $2.00-2.50
❏ ❏   Di9507 **#7 Peter Pan** - in orange boat. $2.00-2.50
❏ ❏   Di9508 **#8 King Louie** - in yellow and green jungle boat. $2.00-2.50

Di9501-04

Di9505-08

HALLOWEEN HAPPY MEAL, 1995

☐ ☐	Ha9501 **#1 Cassette Tape: Ronald Makes it Magic.**		$1.00-1.50
☐ ☐	Ha9502 **#2 Cassette Tape: Travel Tunes.**		$1.00-1.50
☐ ☐	Ha9503 **#3 Cassette Tape: Silly Sing-Along.**		$1.00-1.50
☐ ☐	Ha9504 **#4 Cassette Tape: Scary Sound Effects.**		$1.00-1.50
☐ ☐	Ha9505 **#5 Hamburglar** - with Witch costume. 3 pieces.		$3.00-3.50
☐ ☐	Ha9506 **#6 Grimace** - with Ghost costume. 3 pieces.		$3.00-3.50
☐ ☐	Ha9507 **#7 Ronald** - with Frankenstein costume. 3 pieces.		$3.00-3.50
☐ ☐	Ha9508 **#8 Birdie** - with Pumpkin costume. 3 pieces.		$3.00-3.50

Ha9501-04

Ha9505-08

MUPPET WORKSHOP HAPPY MEAL, 1995

❏ ❏   Mu9501 **#1 Bird Muppet** - turquoise with red hat. 4 pieces. $2.00-2.50
❏ ❏   Mu9502 **#2 Dog Muppet** - pink with orange bird-like hat. 4 pieces. $2.00-2.50
❏ ❏   Mu9503 **#3 Monster Muppet** - green with orange hat and blue bear. 4 pieces.
                     $2.00-2.50

❏ ❏   Mu9504 **#4 What-Not Muppet** - yellow monster with purple cowboy hat and red guitar. 4 pieces. $2.00-2.50

Mu9501-04

POLLY POCKET ATTACK PACK HAPPY MEAL, 1995

❏ ❏   Po9501 **#1 Ring.** Pink and green ring. $2.00-2.50
❏ ❏   Po9502 **#2 Locket.** Pink heart locket. $2.00-2.50
❏ ❏   Po9503 **#3 Stop Watch.** Yellow case stop watch. $2.00-2.50
❏ ❏   Po9504 **#4 Bracelet.** Pink butterfly case bracelet. $2.00-2.50

Po9501-04

Attack Pack Tonka Trucks:

☐ ☐ Hw9505 **#5 Truck** - black dump truck. $2.00-2.50
☐ ☐ Hw9506 **#6 Battle Bird** - green camouflaged colored airplane. $2.00-2.50
☐ ☐ Hw9507 **#7 Lunar Invader.** Yellow and gray Lunar Module. $2.00-2.50
☐ ☐ Hw9508 **#8 Sea Creature** - yellow creature. $2.00-2.50

Hw9505-08

Power Rangers Happy Meal, 1995

☐ ☐ Pr9501 **#1 Power Com** - gray communicator. $2.00-2.50
☐ ☐ Pr9502 **#2 Powermorpher Buckle.** Gray and red belt buckle with 3 gold coins. 4 pieces.
                                                                               $2.00-2.50
☐ ☐ Pr9503 **#3 Power Siren** - black whistle. $2.00-2.50
☐ ☐ Pr9504 **#4 Alien Detector** - purple case with flip open blue door. $2.00-2.50

Pr9501-04

55

Space Rescue Happy Meal, 1995

❏ ❏   Sp9501 **#1 Astro Viewer** - green viewer. $2.00-2.50
❏ ❏   Sp9502 **#2 Tele Communicator** - orange communicator. $2.00-2.50
❏ ❏   Sp9503 **#3 Space Slate** - blue with pink slate. $2.00-2.50
❏ ❏   Sp9504 **#4 Lunar Grabber** - blue, green, and orange handles. $2.00-2.50

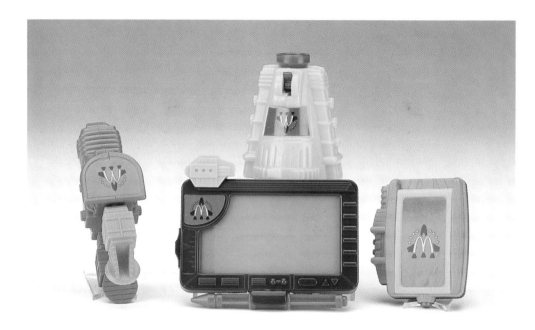

Sp9501-04

Spider-Man Happy Meal, 1995

❑ ❑	Sm9501 **#1 Spider-Man.**		$2.50-3.50
❑ ❑	Sm9502 **#2 Scorpion Stingstriker Green Vehicle.**		$2.50-3.50
❑ ❑	Sm9503 **#3 Dr. Octopus with Gray Tentacles.**		$2.50-3.50
❑ ❑	Sm9504 **#4 Spider-Man in Webrunner.**		$2.50-3.50
❑ ❑	Sm9505 **#5 Mary Jane Watson with Green Clip-on Dress.**		$3.50-5.00
❑ ❑	Sm9506 **#6 Venom Transport Spider Vehicle.**		$2.50-3.50
❑ ❑	Sm9507 **#7 Peter Parker Two Face.**		$2.50-3.50
❑ ❑	Sm9508 **#8 Hobgoblin Land Glider Vehicle.**		$2.50-3.50

Sm9501-04

Sm9505-08

Totally Toy Happy Meal, 1995

☐ ☐ To9501 **#1 Holiday Barbie** - in white and gold sleigh. $3.50-4.00
☐ ☐ To9502 **#2 57 Chevy Hot Wheels or Gator Car** - red or green car with blue ramp.
2 pieces. $2.00-3.50
☐ ☐ To9503 **#3 Polly Pocket House** - in green and pink house with girl inside. $2.00-2.50
☐ ☐ To9504 **#4 Mighty Max Case** - in blue case with Mighty Max figurine inside. $2.00-2.50
☐ ☐ To9505 **#5 Cabbage Patch Kids** - in pink and red rocking horse case. $2.00-2.50
☐ ☐ To9506 **#6 North Pole Explorer Vehicle** - clear case truck. $2.00-2.50
☐ ☐ To9507 **#7 Once Upon A Dream Princess** - red and white dressed figure with white
crown. $2.00-2.50
☐ ☐ To9508 **#8 Knight** - with green dragon. 2 pieces. $2.00-2.50

To9501-04

To9505-08

58

1996

Aladdin and the King of Thieves Happy Meal, 1996

❏	❏	AI9601 **#1 Cassim** - with diorama. 2 pieces.	$2.00-2.50
❏	❏	AI9602 **#2 Abu** - with diorama. 2 pieces.	$2.00-2.50
❏	❏	AI9603 **#3 Jasmine** - with diorama. 2 pieces.	$2.00-2.50
❏	❏	AI9604 **#4 Lago** - with diorama. 2 pieces.	$2.00-2.50
❏	❏	AI9605 **#5 Genie** - with diorama. 2 pieces.	$2.00-2.50
❏	❏	AI9606 **#6 Sa'luk** - with diorama. 2 pieces.	$2.00-2.50
❏	❏	AI9607 **#7 Aladdin** - with diorama. 2 pieces.	$2.00-2.50
❏	❏	AI9608 **#8 Mai Tre D'genie** - with diorama. 2 pieces.	$2.00-2.50

AI9601-03

AI9604-06

AI9607-08

BABE HAPPY MEAL, 1996

❑	❑	Bb9601 **#1 Babe the Pig** - stuffed.	$2.00-2.50
❑	❑	Bb9602 **#2 Cow** - stuffed.	$2.00-2.50
❑	❑	Bb9603 **#3 Maa the Ewe** - stuffed.	$2.00-2.50
❑	❑	Bb9604 **#4 Fly the Dog** - stuffed.	$2.00-2.50
❑	❑	Bb9605 **#5 Ferdinand the Duck** - stuffed.	$2.00-2.50
❑	❑	Bb9606 **#6 Dutchess the Cat** - stuffed.	$2.00-2.50
❑	❑	Bb9607 **#7 Mouse** - stuffed.	$2.00-2.50

Bb9601-04

Bb9605-07

Barbie Dolls of the World and Hot Wheels Happy Meal, 1996

Barbie Dolls:

❑ ❑	Ba9601 **#1 Dutch Barbie** - in blue and white dress.	$1.50-2.50
❑ ❑	Ba9602 **#2 Kenyan Barbie** - in red dress on yellow stand. 2 pieces.	$1.50-2.50
❑ ❑	Ba9603 **#3 Japanese Barbie** - in purple Kimona on black stand.	$1.50-2.50
❑ ❑	Ba9604 **#4 Mexican Barbie** - in red and green dress.	$1.50-2.50
❑ ❑	Ba9605 **#5 U.S.A. Barbie** - in red and blue gymnastic outfit on red stand.	$2.50-2.50

Ba9601-05

Hot Wheel Cars:

☐ ☐	Hw9606 **#6 Flame Hot Wheels** - with metallic blue and orange flames.	$2.50-3.00
☐ ☐	Hw9607 **#7 Roaring Rod Hot Wheels** - with zebra stripes.	$2.50-3.00
☐ ☐	Hw9608 **#8 Dark Rider Batman style Hot Wheels.**	$2.50-3.00
☐ ☐	Hw9609 **#9 Hot Hubs Hot Wheels** - with silver engine.	$2.50-3.00
☐ ☐	Hw9610 **#10 Krackel Car Hot Wheels** - in green and yellow.	$2.50-3.00

Hw9606-10

Eric Carle Finger Puppet Happy Meal, 1996

☐ ☐	Er9601 **#1 The Very Quiet Cricket** - dark blue head with purple body.	$2.00-2.50
☐ ☐	Er9602 **#2 The Grouchy Ladybug** - with red wings.	$2.00-2.50
☐ ☐	Er9603 **#3 The Very Busy Spider** - on white base.	$2.00-2.50
☐ ☐	Er9604 **#4 The Very Hungry Caterpillar** - with red apple.	$2.00-2.50
☐ ☐	Er9605 **#5 A House for Hermit Crab** - red snail in shell.	$2.00-2.50
☐ ☐	Er9606 **#6 The Very Lonely Firefly** - red wings with green head.	$2.00-2.50

Er9601-06

Littlest Pet Shop and Transformers Happy Meal, 1996

☐ ☐   Li9601 **#1 Swan** - with pink wings. $2.00-2.50
☐ ☐   Li9602 **#2 Unicorn** - with pink tail. $2.00-2.50
☐ ☐   Li9603 **#3 Dragon** - with orange wings. $2.00-2.50
☐ ☐   Li9604 **#4 Tiger** - with pink fur. $2.00-2.50

Li9601-04

Transformers:

☐ ☐   Li9605 **#5 Manta Ray.** $2.00-2.50
☐ ☐   Li9606 **#6 Beetle.** $2.00-2.50
☐ ☐   Li9607 **#7 Panther.** $2.00-2.50
☐ ☐   Li9608 **#8 Rhino.** $2.00-2.50

Li9605-08

MARVEL SUPER HEROES HAPPY MEAL, 1996

❑ ❑   Ma9601 **#1 Spider-Man Vehicle.** $2.00-2.50
❑ ❑   Ma9602 **#2 Storm.** $2.00-2.50
❑ ❑   Ma9603 **#3 Wolverine.** $2.00-2.50
❑ ❑   Ma9604 **#4 Jubilee.** $2.00-2.50
❑ ❑   Ma9605 **#5 Invisible Woman.** $2.50-2.50
❑ ❑   Ma9606 **#6 Thing.** $2.00-2.50
❑ ❑   Ma9607 **#7 Hulk.** $2.00-2.50
❑ ❑   Ma9608 **#8 Human Torch.** $2.00-2.50

Ma9601-04

Ma9605-08

Halloween McNugget Buddies Happy Meal, 1996

❏ ❏   Ha9601 **#1 Spider McNugget.** McNugget wearing a purple hat with purple legs. 3 pieces.
$3.00-3.50

❏ ❏   Ha9602 **#2 Rock Star McNugget.** McNugget with a green florescent hat and black shoes as base. 3 pieces. $3.00-3.50

❏ ❏   Ha9603 **#3 Fairy Princess McNugget.** McNugget with yellow hair on metallic green base. 3 pieces. $3.00-3.50

❏ ❏   Ha9604 **#4 Dragon McNugget** - green dragon head and base. 3 pieces. $3.00-3.50

❏ ❏   Ha9605 **#5 Alien Monster McNugget** - orange and green hat with pink base. 3 pieces.
$3.00-3.50

❏ ❏   Ha9606 **#6 Ronald McNugget** - red rock star hair with large red shoes base. 3 pieces.
$3.00-3.50

Ha9601-03

Ha9604-06

65

Muppet Treasure Island Happy Meal, 1996

❏ ❏	Mu9601 **#1 Miss Piggy in green tub.**		$2.00-2.50
❏ ❏	Mu9602 **#2 Kermit in pirate style boat.**		$2.00-2.50
❏ ❏	Mu9603 **#3 Gonzo in purple paddle wheel boat.**		$2.00-2.50
❏ ❏	Mu9604 **#4 Fozzie in blue barrel.**		$2.00-2.50

Mu9601-04

101 Dalmatians Happy Meal, 1996

Dalmatian Figures:

❏ ❏ On9601 **#1 Gold Wrap** - wrapped in gold ribbon. $3.00-4.00

❏ ❏ On9602 **#2 Orange Collar** - orange collar/1 ear spotted. $3.00-4.00

❏ ❏ On9603 **#3 In blue truck** - in blue and brown truck with hiding eyes and light green collar.
    $3.00-4.00

❏ ❏ On9604 **#4 Wearing Brown Derby Hat with blue band** - sitting up/green collar/
brown boller hat with blue hat band. $4.00-5.00

On9601-04

☐ ☐ On9605 **#5 Toy Soldier in Mouth** - orange collar with toy soldier nutcracker/soldier in mouth.
$3.00-4.00

☐ ☐ On9606 **#6 Dark Blue Collar / I Black Ear** - dark blue collar/1 all black ear/1 spotted
ear. $3.00-4.00

☐ ☐ On9607 **#7 Green Wreath on tail** - light green collar with green wreath on rump.
$3.00-4.00

☐ ☐ On9608 **#8 Holly Flower On Tail / Pink Collar** - standing/pink collar/green holly with
yellow jingle bells on tail. 3.00-4.00

☐ ☐ On9609 **#9 Pink Collar / 2 Black Ears** - fuchsia collar/2 solid black ears. $3.00-4.00

☐ ☐ On9610 **#10 Wearing Cowboy Hat** - dark green collar/brown cowboy hat with red
band. $5.00-8.00

☐ ☐ On9611 **#11 In Pink Tea Pot.** $8.00-10.00

☐ ☐ On9612 **#12 Blue Mitten in Mouth** - yellow collar. $3.00-4.00

On9605-8

On9609-12

67

❏ ❏ On9613 **#13 Newspaper in Mouth** - green collar. $3.00-4.00
❏ ❏ On9614 **#14 Wrapped in Yellow/Green Scarf/sweater** - no collar. $3.00-4.00
❏ ❏ On9615 **#15 Brown Bucket on tail** - orange collar. $3.00-4.00
❏ ❏ On9616 **#16 Wearing Green Santa Hat/Holding Bone** - standing/blue collar.
$3.00-4.00
❏ ❏ On9617 **#17 Plain Green Collar** - mouth open/spotted ears. $3.00-4.00
❏ ❏ On9618 **#18 In Pink Baby Buggy** - with turquoise wheels/blue collar/hiding eyes.
$5.00-8.00
❏ ❏ On9619 **#19 In Newspaper** - in white london herald newspaper house. $5.00-8.00
❏ ❏ On9620 **#20 Wrapped in Red Scarf with Yellow** - sweater/scarf with yellow tassels.
$3.00-4.00

On9613-16

On9617-20

68

❏ ❏ On9621 **#21 Christmas Lights Wrapped Around Face** - blue collar/sitting/red christmas lights around face. $3.00-4.00

❏ ❏ On9622 **#22 Dog on 101 Drum** - on heavy red 101 dalmatian drum/purple collar. $8.00-10.00

❏ ❏ On9623 **#23 Plain Yellow Collar** - yellow collar/spotted ears. $3.00-4.00

❏ ❏ On9624 **#24 Black Rings Around Eye** - dark purple collar/black eye/2 solid black ears. $3.00-4.00

❏ ❏ On9625 **#25 In Red Present** - orange collar. $3.00-4.00

❏ ❏ On9626 **#26 Candy Cane in Mouth** - sitting with red/white candy cane in mouth/sitting/ green collar. $3.00-4.00

❏ ❏ On9627 **#27 Holding Red Book on belly** - holding red book/green collar/black eye. $3.00-4.00

❏ ❏ On9628 **#28 In Yellow Cookie Jar** - green collar. $5.00-8.00

On9621-24

On9625-28

69

❏ ❏ On9629 **#29 Brown Shoe in Mouth** - holding brown shoe in mouth/purple collar/1 solid black ear. $3.00-4.00

❏ ❏ On9630 **#30 In Yellow Present** - coming out of yellow present/blue collar/red santa hat. $3.00-4.00

❏ ❏ On9631 **#31 With Green Candy Cane in Mouth/Holding Bone** - standing with purple collar. $3.00-4.00

❏ ❏ On9632 **#32 Light Blue Collar/White Ear** - right paw up with 1 spotted ear. $3.00-4.00

❏ ❏ On9633 **#33 In Red Stocking** - green collar/white bone in mouth/black eye. $3.00-4.00

❏ ❏ On9634 **#34 Wearing Black Cruella Hat** - sitting with red collar. $3.00-4.00

❏ ❏ On9635 **#35 Plain Purple Collar/White Ears** - dark purple collar/1 white ear. $3.00-4.00

❏ ❏ On9636 **#36 Bluebird on Head** - red-orange collar. $5.00-8.00

On9629-32

On9633-36

70

☐ ☐ On9637 **#37 Wrapped in Blue Scarf** - purple tassels. $3.00-4.00
☐ ☐ On9638 **#38 In White DeVil Car** - orange collar. $5.00-8.00
☐ ☐ On9639 **#39 Yellow Bow on Tail** - standing/purple collar/one black foot. $3.00-4.00
☐ ☐ On9640 **#40 In Green Wreaths with Red Bow** - wearing red santa hat/blue collar.
                                                                                         $3.00-4.00
☐ ☐ On9641 **#41 Holding Cookie** - standing with blue collar. $3.00-4.00
☐ ☐ On9642 **#42 Tennis Shoe in Mouth** - laying flat/black-white tennis shoe in mouth/blue
        collar. $3.00-4.00
☐ ☐ On9643 **#43 On Red Ornament** - on heavy red christmas ball decorated with green
        tree/yellow collar. $5.00-8.00
☐ ☐ On9644 **#44 Wearing Indiana Jones Hat** - with dark pink collar. $5.00-8.00
☐ ☐ On9645 **#45 Candle in Mouth** - with orange candle in mouth/dark purple collar.
                                                                                         $3.00-4.00

On9637-41

On9642-45

71

❏ ❏ On9646 **#46 Wrapped in Green Ribbon** - I black ear/no collar. $3.00-4.00
❏ ❏ On9647 **#47 Teddy Bear on Stomach** - laying with yellow teddy bear on stomach/ orange collar. $7.00-10.00
❏ ❏ On9648 **#48 In Green Bus** - with purple collar. $3.00-5.00
❏ ❏ On9649 **#49 Wrapped in Silver Ribbon** - 2 spots on one ear/no collar. $3.00-4.00
❏ ❏ On9650 **#50 In Lavender Book** - with purple book. $7.00-10.00
❏ ❏ On9651 **#51 Wearing Mickey Mouse Ears** - with "Fidget" name back of hat/light blue collar. $7.00-10.00
❏ ❏ On9652 **#52 In Blue Baby Buggy** - with yellow wheels/red collar. $5.00-8.00

On9646-49

On9650-52

72

❏ ❏	On9653 **#53 Wrapped in Aqua Garland** - with purple ornaments/spotted head/no collar.	$3.00-4.00
❏ ❏	On9654 **#54 Wrapped in Green Wreath with Yellow Ribbon** - with candy cane in mouth.	$3.00-4.00
❏ ❏	On9655 **#55 Wearing Blue Bobby Hat** - with red collar.	$3.00-4.00
❏ ❏	On9656 **#56 Wearing Crown on Head** - with lavender collar.	$5.00-8.00
❏ ❏	On9657 **#57 In Red Bus** - with light green collar.	$3.00-4.00
❏ ❏	On9658 **#58 In Bobby Hat** - with red collar.	$5.00-8.00
❏ ❏	On9659 **#59 Yellow Trumpet on Stomach** - laying down/playing yellow trumpet/horn/ holly on horn/red collar.	$3.00-4.00
❏ ❏	On9660 **#60 Wrapped in Red Garland** - with green ornaments/no collar.	$3.00-4.00

On9653-56

On9657-60

73

❏ ❏ On9661 **#61 In Blue Present** - with bone in mouth/silver ribbon/purple collar.
$3.00-4.00

❏ ❏ On9662 **#62 Leash Wrapped Around Face** - with green collar. $3.00-5.00
❏ ❏ On9663 **#63 In Silver Paint Can** - with purple paint. $5.00-8.00
❏ ❏ On9664 **#64 Holding bone in mouth** - with light green collar. $3.00-4.00
❏ ❏ on9665 **#65 On Soccer Ball** - with yellow collar. $5.00-8.00
❏ ❏ On9666 **#66 Solid Black Tail Painted On** - with fuchsia/red collar/no spots on ears.
$3.00-4.00

❏ ❏ On9667 **#67 Holding Dog Dish in mouth** - with green collar. $3.00-4.00
❏ ❏ On9668 **#68 Green Frog on Head** - with pink/fuchsia collar. $5.00-8.00

On9661-64

On9665-68

❑ ❑	On9669 **#69 Blue Top Hat on Tail** - with green collar.	$3.00-4.00
❑ ❑	On9670 **#70 Butterfly on Head** - with green/teal collar.	$5.00-8.00
❑ ❑	On9671 **#71 Red Flower/bow on Nose** - with yellow collar.	$3.00-4.00
❑ ❑	On9672 **#72 Holding Blue Can of Dog Treats** - with yellow collar.	$3.00-4.00
❑ ❑	On9673 **#73 Red Bow on tail** - with blue collar.	$3.00-4.00
❑ ❑	On9674 **#74 Holding Red Dog Dish** - with purple collar.	$3.00-4.00
❑ ❑	On9675 **#75 Stick in mouth** - with pinkish-lavender collar.	$3.00-4.00
❑ ❑	On9676 **#76 In Red Doghouse** - with green roof.	$3.00-4.00

On9669-72

On9673-76

❏ ❏ On9677 **#77 Holding Purple Present** - with lime green collar. $3.00-4.00
❏ ❏ On9678 **#78 In Green Stocking** - with red-white candy cane in mouth/blue collar.
                                                                        $3.00-4.00
❏ ❏ On9679 **#79 Wearing Black Palace Hat** - with purple collar. $3.00-4.00
❏ ❏ On9680 **#80 Leash in mouth** - with orange collar. $3.00-4.00
❏ ❏ On9681 **#81 Holding Green Bell** - with red holly/fuchsia collar. $3.00-4.00
❏ ❏ On9682 **#82 Purple Bow on Head** - with blue collar. $3.00-4.00
❏ ❏ On9683 **#83 In Brownish red Barrel** - with blue collar. $3.00-4.00
❏ ❏ On9684 **#84 In Purple Umbrella** - with green collar. $8.00-10.00

On9677-80

On9681-84

❏	❏	On9685 **#85 Wearing Gray Wig** - with fuchsia collar.	$4.00-5.00
❏	❏	On9686 **#86 On Green Turtle** - with red-orange collar.	$8.00-10.00
❏	❏	On9687 **#87 Pushing Blue and White Soccer Ball** - with orange collar.	$3.00-4.00
❏	❏	On9688 **#88 Red Ornament on Nose** - with purple collar.	$3.00-4.00
❏	❏	On9689 **#89 Orange Maple Leaf on Head** - with fuchsia collar.	$3.00-4.00
❏	❏	On9690 **#90 Wearing Green Santa Stocking** - with red collar.	$3.00-4.00
❏	❏	On9691 **#91 Wearing Purple Beret** - with yellow collar.	$4.00-5.00
❏	❏	On9692 **#92 in black rubber tire** - with red collar.	$5.00-8.00
❏	❏	On9693 **#93 Wearing Blue Baseball Cap** - with orange collar.	$3.00-4.00

On9685-89

On9690-93

❏	❏	On9694 **#94 Gold Present in Mouth** - with blue collar.	$3.00-4.00
❏	❏	On9695 **#95 Green Wreath around Nose** - with yellow collar.	$3.00-4.00
❏	❏	On9696 **#96 Green Cricket on Head** - with purple collar.	$5.00-8.00
❏	❏	On9697 **#97 Pink Present on Tail** - with yellow collar.	$3.00-4.00
❏	❏	On9698 **#98 Brown Purse in Mouth** - with red collar.	$3.00-4.00
❏	❏	On9699 **#99 Red Santa Hat on Tail** - with purple collar.	$3.00-4.00
❏	❏	On96100 **#100 Wearing Orange Hunting Cap** - with lime green collar.	$3.00-4.00
❏	❏	On96101 **#101 In Red Car** - with purple collar.	$3.00-4.00

On9694-97

On9698-101

78

Space Jam Happy Meal, 1996

☐ ☐   Sp9601 **#1 Lola Bunny** - lady basketball player. $2.00-2.50
☐ ☐   Sp9602 **#2 Bugs Bunny** - shooting basket. $2.00-2.50
☐ ☐   Sp9603 **#3 Marvin the Martian** - on top of orange ball. $2.00-2.50
☐ ☐   Sp9604 **#4 Daffy Duck** - standing on top of orange ball. $2.00-2.50
☐ ☐   Sp9605 **#5 Tasmanian Devil** - shooting ball into white hoop. $2.00-2.50
☐ ☐   Sp9606 **#6 Monstar** - green player with arms raised. $2.00-2.50
☐ ☐   Sp9607 **#7 Sylvester & Tweety** - on orange ball. $2.00-2.50
☐ ☐   Sp9608 **#8 Nerdlucks** - purple/blue totem pole style player on brown base. $2.00-2.50

Sp9601-04

Sp9605-08

VR Troopers Happy Meal, 1996

☐ ☐   Vr9601 **#1 Visor** - silver glasses. $2.00-2.50
☐ ☐   Vr9602 **#2 Virtualizer Pendant.** $2.00-2.50
☐ ☐   Vr9603 **#3 Wrist Spinner with 2 disc.** 3 pieces. $2.00-2.50
☐ ☐   Vr9604 **#4 Kaleidoscope shaped like a camera.** $2.00-2.50

Vr9601-04

Walt Disney Home Video Happy Meal, 1996

☐ ☐   Wa9601 **#1 Cinderella.** $3.00-4.00
☐ ☐   Wa9602 **#2 Robin Hood with Gold Money Bag.** $3.00-4.00
☐ ☐   Wa9603 **#3 Pocahontas with orange comb.** $3.00-4.00
☐ ☐   Wa9604 **#4 Aladdin.** $3.00-4.00

Wa9601-04

❑	❑	Wa9605 **#5 Snow White.**	$3.00-4.00
❑	❑	Wa9606 **#6 Merlin.**	$3.00-4.00
❑	❑	Wa9607 **#7 Alice in Wonderland with purple comb.**	$3.00-4.00
❑	❑	Wa9608 **#8 Scat the Cat.**	$3.00-4.00

Wa9605-08

1997

ANIMAL PALS HAPPY MEAL, 1997

❑	❑	An9701 **#1 Panda** - stuffed.	$2.00-2.50
❑	❑	An9702 **#2 Rhinoceros** - stuffed.	$2.00-2.50
❑	❑	An9703 **#3 Yak** - stuffed.	$2.00-2.50
❑	❑	An9704 **#4 Moose** - stuffed.	$2.00-2.50
❑	❑	An9705 **#5 Brown Bear** - stuffed.	$2.00-2.50
❑	❑	An9706 **#6 Gorilla** - stuffed.	$2.00-2.50

An9701-06

BARBIE AND HOT WHEELS HAPPY MEAL, 1997

BARBIE DOLLS:

□ □ Ba9701 **#1 Wedding Bride Rapunzel Barbie** - with white dress and gold trim on white heart shaped doll stand. 2 pieces. $2.00-2.50

□ □ Ba9702 **#2 Rapunzel Barbie** - with pink dress and gold trim on gray circle shaped doll stand. 2 pieces. $2.00-2.50

□ □ Ba9703 **#3 Angel Princess Barbie** - with long white dress and pedal shaped wings on pink doll stand. 2 pieces. $2.00-2.50

□ □ Ba9704 **#4 Happy Holidays Barbie** - with red and white long dress on green wreath shaped doll stand. 2 pieces. $2.00-2.50

□ □ Ba9705 **#5 Blossom Beauty African American Barbie** - in floral dress on yellow flower pedal doll stand. 2 pieces. $2.00-2.50

Ba9701-05

HOT WHEELS CARS:

□ □ Hw9706 **#6 Tow truck** - dark blue with yellow bumper. $2.00-2.50

□ □ Hw9707 **#7 Taxi car** - yellow taxi with black spoiler. $2.00-2.50

□ □ Hw9708 **#8 Police car** - black/white police car with 1968 gold star on hood. $2.00-2.50

□ □ Hw9709 **#9 Ambulance van** - white ambulance with red flashing-type lights with Red Cross symbol on side. $2.00-2.50

□ □ Hw9710 **#10 Fire truck** - red fire truck with gray extension hose on top. $2.00-2.50

Hw9706-10

❑ ❑ Be9701 **#1 Beetle Bonder** - with black wings and claws. $1.50-2.00
❑ ❑ Be9702 **#2 Chromium Gold Compact.** $1.50-2.00
❑ ❑ Be9703 **#3 Hunter Claw** - with orange hands. $1.50-2.00
❑ ❑ Be9704 **#4 Platinum Purple Compact.** $1.50-2.00
❑ ❑ Be9705 **#5 Stinger Drill** - shaped like a cone. $1.50-2.00
❑ ❑ Be9706 **#6 Silver Compact Wristband.** $1.50-2.00

Be9701-03

Be9704-06

HERCULES HAPPY MEAL, 1997

❏ ❏ He9701 **#1 Wind Titan & Hermes** - blue figure in gray case. 3 pieces. $2.00-2.50
❏ ❏ He9702 **#2 Rock Titan & Zeus** - orange and purple figure in brown case. 3 pieces.
$2.00-2.50
❏ ❏ He9703 **#3 Hydra & Hercules** - brown figure with gold shield in purple case. 3 pieces
$2.00-2.50
❏ ❏ He9704 **#4 Lava Titan & Baby Pegasus** - white and blue baby horse in red case. 3 pieces.
$2.00-2.50
❏ ❏ He9705 **#5 Cyclops & Pain** - purple figure with large white teeth in cream case. 3 pieces.
$2.00-2.50
❏ ❏ He9706 **#6 Fates & Panic** - turquoise figure with white eyeball in gray case. 3 pieces.
$2.00-2.50
❏ ❏ He9707 **#7 Pegasus & Megara** - female figure with purple dress and long hair in white
horse case. 3 pieces. $2.00-2.50
❏ ❏ He9708 **#8 Ice Titan & Calliope** - female figure with purple dress with short brown
hair in clear case. 3 pieces. $2.00-2.50
❏ ❏ He9709 **#9 Nessus & Phil** - tan figure with dark purple case. $2.00-2.50
❏ ❏ He9710 **#10 Cerberus & Hades** - blue and gray figure with eye in 3 headed case. 3 pieces.
$2.00-2.50

He9701-03

84

He9704-06

He9707-10

❑	❑	Hu9701 **#1 Esmeralda amulet necklace.**	$2.00-2.50
❑	❑	Hu9702 **#2 Scepter.**	$2.00-2.50
❑	❑	Hu9703 **#3 Clopin Mask.**	$2.00-2.50
❑	❑	Hu9704 **#4 Hugo Horn.**	$2.00-2.50
❑	❑	Hu9705 **#5 Three Juggling Balls.** 3 pieces.	$2.00-2.50
❑	❑	Hu9706 **#6 Jester with purple hat on Drum.**	$2.00-2.50
❑	❑	Hu9707 **#7 Quasimodo Bird Catcher.**	$2.00-2.50
❑	❑	Hu9708 **#8 Tambourine.**	$2.00-2.50

Hu9701-04

Hu9705-08

Jungle Book Happy Meal, 1997

☐ ☐	Ju9701 **#1 Baloo** - Bear holding yellow bunch of bananas.		$2.50-3.00
☐ ☐	Ju9702 **#2 Junior** - Elephant.		$2.50-3.00
☐ ☐	Ju9703 **#3 Bagheera** - Cheta.		$2.50-3.00
☐ ☐	Ju9704 **#4 King Louie** - Monkey.		$2.50-3.00
☐ ☐	Ju9705 **#5 Kaa** - Snake on palm tree.		$2.50-3.00
☐ ☐	Ju9706 **#6 Mowgli** - Boy with coconuts.		$2.50-3.00

Ju9701-03

Ju9704-06

LITTLE MERMAID HAPPY MEAL, 1997

❏ ❏   Li9701 **#1 Ursula** - black and purple Ursula blow-up floater with gray ring. 2 pieces.
                                                                   $2.50-3.50
❏ ❏   Li9702 **#2 Flounder** - yellow and blue fish floater. $2.50-3.50
❏ ❏   Li9703 **#3 Scuttle** - white bird with orange. $2.50-3.50
❏ ❏   Li9704 **#4 Ariel** - Mermaid with red hair holding seahorse. $2.50-3.50
❏ ❏   Li9705 **#5 Max** - gray sea animal with 2 arms. $2.50-3.50
❏ ❏   Li9706 **#6 Glut** - gray shark. $2.50-3.50
❏ ❏   Li9707 **#7 Eric** - Prince Eric in boat. $2.50-3.50
❏ ❏   Li9708 **#8 Sebastian** - red crab. $2.50-3.50

Li9701-04

Li9705-08

Mighty Ducks Happy Meal, 1997

☐ ☐   Mi9701 **#1 Wildwing** - black hockey puck. $2.00-2.50
☐ ☐   Mi9702 **#2 Nosedive** - purple hockey puck. $2.00-2.50
☐ ☐   Mi9703 **#3 Mallory** - yellow hockey puck. $2.00-2.50
☐ ☐   Mi9704 **#4 Duke L'orange** - blue hockey puck. $2.00-2.50

Mi9701-04

❑ ❑ On9701 **#1 Gray Dalmatian** - in orange and blue flip car with pink wheels. $2.00-2.50

❑ ❑ On9702 **#2 White Dalmatian** - with 2 black ears in yellow and purple flip car with black and orange wheels. $2.00-2.50

❑ ❑ On9703 **#3 White Dalmatian** - with 2 black ears and red collar in gray and orange flip car with black and green wheels. $2.00-2.50

❑ ❑ On9704 **#4 White Dalmatian** - with spotted ears and blue collar in light purple and gray flip car with orange and blue wheels. $2.00-2.50

❑ ❑ On9705 **#5 Green Dalmatian** - in blue and purple flip car with yellow and orange wheels. $2.00-2.50

❑ ❑ On9706 **#6 Pink Dalmatian** - in orange and green flip car with white and blue wheels. $2.00-2.50

❑ ❑ On9707 **#7 White Dalmatian** - with blue collar in blue and yellow flip car with green and purple wheels. $2.00-2.50

❑ ❑ On9708 **#8 Gray Dalmatian** - in yellow and purple flip car with red and tan wheels. $2.00-2.50

On9701-04

On9705-08

❏ ❏   Sk9701 **#1 Swan Shimmer** - brown face with orange wings on light blue base. 2 pieces.
$2.00-2.50

❏ ❏   Sk9702 **#2 Rosemerry Rosemarie** - white face with lime green wings with dark purple base. $2.00-2.50

❏ ❏   Sk9703 **#3 Flutterfly Luciole** - white face with light yellow wings with turquoise base. 2 pieces. $2.00-2.50

❏ ❏   Sk9704 **#4 Princess Pegus - Princess Pivoine** - white face with pink wings with light purple base. 2 pieces. $2.00-2.50

❏ ❏   Sk9705 **#5 Evac Copter** - gold helicopter body with black wings on red base.
$2.00-2.50

❏ ❏   Sk9706 **#6 Polar Explorer Vehicle** - light purple and silver body with red and blue front bumper and antennae on roof. $2.00-2.50

❏ ❏   Sk9707 **#7 Deep Sea Hunter Sea Crane** - gray crane with metallic orange body on a blue base. $2.00-2.50

❏ ❏   Sk9708 **#8 Ocean Flyer Airplane Sea Plane** - silver body with black props on a red base. $2.00-2.50

Sk9701-04

Sk9705-08

Sleeping Beauty Happy Meal, 1997

❑ ❑   Usa SI9701 **#1 Sleeping Beauty Pencil Cap & Eraser.** Sleeping Beauty with long blue
         dress with yellow spinning wheel eraser. 2 pieces. $3.00-3.50

❑ ❑   Usa SI9702 **#2 Maleficent with Green Ruler.** Maleficent wearing a black cape with a green
         ruler. 2 pieces. $3.00-3.50

❑ ❑   Usa SI9703 **#3 Prince Philip with Paint Brush & Palette.** Gray and black dressed
         Prince holding blue shield with paper palette and gray sword as paint brush. 3 pieces.
            $3.00-3.50

❑ ❑   Usa SI9704 **#4 Flora Paper Punch.** Orange and gray rolly polly Flora with paper punch
         on bottom. $3.00-3.50

❑ ❑   Usa SI9705 **#5 Dragon Ink Pen.** Black and gray dragon as ink pen. $3.00-3.50

❑ ❑   Usa SI9706 **#6 Raven Book Clip.** Black Raven with wings as book clip. $3.00-3.50

Usa SI9701-06

TANGLE TWIST-A-TOID HAPPY MEAL, 1997

❑ ❑ Ta9701 **#1 Purple and Pink 3-Legged Creature** - with 2 long pink and 2 short pink twists. 5 pieces. $1.50-2.00

❑ ❑ Ta9702 **#2 Lime Green Creature** - with 2 long orange and 2 short orange twists. 5 pieces. $1.50-2.00

❑ ❑ Ta9703 **#3 Red body with Gold-Eyed Headed Standing Creature** - with 2 long purple and 2 short purple twists. 5 pieces. $1.50-2.00

❑ ❑ Ta9704 **#4 Gold Body Creature with 3 Legs** - with 2 lime green and 1 blue plus 1 orange twist. 5 pieces. $1.50-2.00

❑ ❑ Ta9705 **#5 Purple Body Creature with Lime Green Eyes** - with 1 long green and 1 short green plus 1 gold short and 1 pink short twist. 5 pieces. $1.50-2.00

❑ ❑ Ta9706 **#6 Orange Body and Purple Legged Creature** - with 1 long gold and 1 short gold plus 1 long green and 1 purple short twist. 5 pieces. $1.50-2.00

❑ ❑ Ta9707 **#7 Green Body Creature** - standing with 1 long purple and 1 short purple plus 1 short green and 1 short purple twist. 5 pieces. $1.50-2.00

❑ ❑ Ta9708 **#8 Blue Blow Fish Creature** - with 1 long orange and 1 short orange plus 1 long blue and 1 short purple twist. 5 pieces. $1.50-2.00

Ta9701-04

Ta9705-08

TEENIE BEANIE BABIES HAPPY MEAL, 1997

❏ ❏ Ty9701 **#1 Patti Platypus** - purple stuffed playpus with gold beak and feet. $10.00-15.00
❏ ❏ Ty9702 **#2 Chops Lamb** - white stuffed lamb with black face. $8.00-10.00
❏ ❏ Ty9703 **#3 Goldie Goldfish** - orange with red tale stripe. $5.00-8.00
❏ ❏ Ty9704 **#4 Seamore Seal** - white seal with black eyes. $5.00-8.00
❏ ❏ Ty9705 **#5 Quacks Duck** - yellow duck with gold beak and feet. $5.00-8.00
❏ ❏ Ty9706 **#6 Pinky Flamingo** - pink flamingo with gold beak. $8.00-10.00
❏ ❏ Ty9707 **#7 Chocolate Moose** - brown moose with gold antlers. $5.00-8.00
❏ ❏ Ty9708 **#8 Speedy Turtle** - green turtle with brown shell. $5.00-8.00
❏ ❏ Ty9709 **#9 Snort Bull** - red bull with white hoofs. $5.00-8.00
❏ ❏ Ty9710 **#10 Lizzy Lizard** - blue lizard with black spots and gold stomach. $5.00-8.00

Ty9701-03

Ty9704-06

94

Ty9707, 08, 10

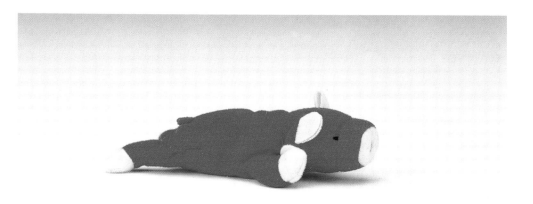

Ty9709

WALT DISNEY HOME VIDEO HAPPY MEAL, 1997

❑ ❑   Wa9701 #1 Bambi with Video Box. $3.00-3.50
❑ ❑   Wa9702 #2 Simba from The Lion King with Video Box. $3.00-3.50
❑ ❑   Wa9703 #3 Elliott from Pete's Dragon with Video Box. $3.00-3.50
❑ ❑   Wa9704 #4 Dodger from Oliver & Company with Video Box. $3.00-3.50
❑ ❑   Wa9705 #5 Princess Aurora from Sleeping Beauty with Video Box. $3.00-3.50
❑ ❑   Wa9706 #6 Woody from Toy Story with Video Box. $3.00-3.50
❑ ❑   Wa9707 #7 Donald Duck from The Three Caballeros with Video Box. $3.00-3.50
❑ ❑   Wa9708 #8 Tigger from Winnie the Pooh with Video Box. $3.00-3.50

Wa9701-04

Wa9705-08

1998

ANIMAL KINGDOM HAPPY MEAL, 1998

❏ ❏ An9801 **#1 Triceratops.** Green dinosaur with 2 white horns. $2.00-2.50
❏ ❏ An9802 **#2 Toucan.** Black and yellow bird. $2.00-2.50
❏ ❏ An9803 **#3 Gorilla & Baby Gorilla on pole.** Black gorilla holding baby on brown pole.
                                                                                                      $2.00-2.50
❏ ❏ An9804 **#4 Elephant.** Gray elephant with tusks. $2.00-2.50
❏ ❏ An9805 **#5 Ring Tail Lemur.** Brown lemur with white head & black striped tale.
                                                                                                      $2.00-2.50
❏ ❏ An9806 **#6 Dragon.** Purple dragon with long purple and black wings. $2.00-2.50
❏ ❏ An9807 **#7 Iguanodon.** Turquoise iguana with purple shading. $2.00-2.50
❏ ❏ An9808 **#8 Zebra.** Black and white striped animal. $2.00-2.50

An9801-04

An9805-08

☐ ☐	An9809 **#9 Lion.** Yellow and brown lion.	$2.00-2.50
☐ ☐	An9810 **#10 Cheetah.** Yellow and black animal.	$2.00-2.50
☐ ☐	An9811 **#11 Crocodile.** Green crocodile with open mouth.	$2.00-2.50
☐ ☐	An9812 **#12 Rhino.** Gray rhino with 2 horns.	$2.00-2.50

An9809-12

BARBIE AND HOT WHEELS HAPPY MEAL, 1998

BARBIE DOLLS:

☐ ☐ Usa Ba9801 **#1 Teen Skipper** - wearing green overalls on pink hear shaped base.
$2.00-2.50

☐ ☐ Usa Ba9802 **#2 Nineties Barbie** - wearing denim jeans and jacket with red shirt on red round base.
$2.00-2.50

☐ ☐ Usa Ba9803 **#3 Eating Fun Kelly** - baby in blue and white high chair. $2.00-2.50

☐ ☐ Usa Ba9804 **#4 Bead Blast Christie** - pink and white striped dress and beads in hair.
$2.00-2.50

Usa Ba9801-04

HOT WHEEL CARS:

☐ ☐ Hw9805 **#5 Ronald NASCAR** - red car with Ronald's Face on hood. $2.00-2.50
☐ ☐ Hw9806 **#6 Mac Tonight Car** - blue with Mac Tonight on hood. $2.00-2.50
☐ ☐ Hw9807 **#7 Hot Wheels NASCAR** - blue car with Hot Wheels on hood. $2.00-2.50
☐ ☐ Hw9808 **#8 50th Anniversary Car** - silver with 50th Anniversary on the hood.
$2.00-2.50

Hw9805-08

A Bug's Life Happy Meal, 1998

❏	❏	Bu9801 **#1 Dim** - blue beetle bug with blue shell.	$2.00-2.50
❏	❏	Bu9802 **#2 Rosie** - purple six legged spider.	$2.00-2.50
❏	❏	Bu9803 **#3 Dot** - purple bug on blue mushroom.	$2.00-2.50
❏	❏	Bu9804 **#4 Flik** - purple bug with green backpack on green leaf.	$2.00-2.50
❏	❏	Bu9805 **#5 Francis** - gray, black, and red beetle standing up.	$2.00-2.50
❏	❏	Bu9806 **#6 Heimlich** - green snail.	$2.00-2.50
❏	❏	Bu9807 **#7 Hopper** - tan grasshopper.	$2.00-2.50
❏	❏	Bu9808 **#8 Atta** - purple fly on green leaf.	$2.00-2.50

Bu9801-04

Bu9805-08

100

DISNEY VIDEO FAVORITES HAPPY MEAL, 1998

☐ ☐	Di9801 **#1 Mickey Mouse on Video Box.**	$2.00-2.50
☐ ☐	Di9802 **#2 Lady and the Tramp on Video Box.**	$2.00-2.50
☐ ☐	Di9803 **#3 Pocahontas: Journey to a New World on Video Box.**	$2.00-2.50
☐ ☐	Di9804 **#4 Mary Poppins on Video Box** - penguin on box.	$2.00-2.50
☐ ☐	Di9805 **#5 The Black Cauldron on Video Box** - tan animal figure on box.	$2.00-2.50
☐ ☐	Di9806 **#6 Flubber on Video Box** - green figure with black sunglasses on box.	
		$2.00-2.50

Di9801-03

Di9804-06

HAUNTED HALLOWEEN HAPPY MEAL, 1998

❏ ❏ Ha9801 **#1 Iam Hungry.** Green character with purple witch's face. 2 pieces.
$2.00-2.50

❏ ❏ Ha9802 **#2 Birdie.** Pink character with black cat's face with blue bow. 2 pieces.
$2.00-2.50

❏ ❏ Ha9803 **#3 Grimace.** Purple character with orange pumpkin face. 2 pieces.
$2.00-2.50

❏ ❏ Ha9804 **#4 McNugget Buddy.** Brown Chicken McNugget with white ghost face. 2 pieces.
$2.00-2.50

❏ ❏ Ha9805 **#5 Ronald.** Red Ronald with blue spooky face and purple hat. 2 pieces.
$2.00-2.50

❏ ❏ Ha9806 **#6 Hamburglar.** Black character with green ghost face and purple spider on tongue. 2 pieces.
$2.00-2.50

Ha9801-03

Ha9804-06

HERCULES HAPPY MEAL, 1998

❑ ❑　He9801 **#1 Zeus Football** - orange mini football with Zeus' face in white.　$2.00-2.50
❑ ❑　He9802 **#2 Hades Stopwatch** - blue, gray and yellow plastic clock shaped stopwatch.
　　　　　　　　　　　　　　　　　　　　　　　　　　　　　　　　　　　$2.00-2.50
❑ ❑　He9803 **#3 Hercules Sports Bottle** - blue column shaped bottle with Hercules' picture.
　　　　　　　　　　　　　　　　　　　　　　　　　　　　　　　　　　　$2.00-2.50
❑ ❑　He9804 **#4 Eyes of Fates Foot Bag** - white bean bag with eye imprint.　$2.00-2.50
❑ ❑　He9805 **#5 Pegasus Whistling Discus** - silver disc.　$2.00-2.50
❑ ❑　He9806 **#6 Pain and Panic Sound Baton** - purple column shaped sound stick.
　　　　　　　　　　　　　　　　　　　　　　　　　　　　　　　　　　　$2.00-2.50
❑ ❑　He9807 **#7 Hercules Medal** - silver and black locket opening to Hercules' picture.
　　　　　　　　　　　　　　　　　　　　　　　　　　　　　　　　　　　$2.00-2.50
❑ ❑　He9808 **#8 Phil Megaphone** - purple with yellow handle.　$2.00-2.50

He9801-03

He9804-08

My Little Pony and Transformers Happy Meal, 1998

My Little Pony Figurines:
❏ ❏   My9801 **#1 Ivy Pony** - turquoise pony with pink tail and purple mane. $2.00-3.00
❏ ❏   My9802 **#2 Sundance Pony** - pink pony with pink tail and yellow sunburst on rump including a blue and pink mane. $2.00-3.00
❏ ❏   My9803 **#3 Light Heart Pony** - white pony with pink heart on rump and purple with beige tail. $2.00-3.00

Transformers:
❏ ❏   My9804 **#4 Scorponok** - purple, blue, and gray crablike figure with crab claws.
   $2.00-2.50
❏ ❏   My9805 **#5 Blackarachnia** - purple body with blue mask and orange claws forming a beetlelike figure. $2.00-2.50
❏ ❏   My9806 **#6 Dinobot** - blue, silver, and green serpent-like figure having a green head mask. $2.00-2.50

My9801-03

My9804-06

Mulan Happy Meal, 1998

❏ ❏   Mu9801 **#1 Mulan** - girl with purple apron sporting black and green armor. 2 pieces.
                                                                         $1.00-1.50

❏ ❏   Mu9802 **#2 Cri-Kee** - purple cricket. $1.00-1.50

❏ ❏   Mu9803 **#3 Khan** - black horse with yellow saddle. $1.00-1.50

❏ ❏   Mu9804 **#4 Shan-Yu** - samurai warrior with sword. $1.00-1.50

❏ ❏   Mu9805 **#5 Little Brother** - white dog. $1.00-1.50

❏ ❏   Mu9806 **#6 Shang-Li** - male samurai warrior with green jacket. $1.00-1.50

❏ ❏   Mu9807 **#7 Mushu** - dragon with gold gong. $1.00-1.50

❏ ❏   Mu9808 **#8 Chien-Po & Ling, Yao** - summo wrestler with figure on rope. 2 pieces.
                                                                      $1.00-1.50

Mu9801-05

Mu9806-08

PETER PAN HAPPY MEAL, 1998

❏ ❏   Pe9801 **#1 Peter Pan Glider** - with green clothes attached to clear wings. $2.00-2.50

❏ ❏   Pe9802 **#2 Tick Tock Crocodile Compass** - green compass in fliptop mouth.
                                                    $2.00-2.50

❏ ❏   Pe9803 **#3 Captain Hook Spyglass** - red spy glass with Captain Hook's head and arm
on handle. $2.00-2.50

❏ ❏   Pe9804 **#4 Wendy & Michael Magnifier** - Wendy & Michael figures imprinted on green
magnifier. $2.00-2.50

❏ ❏   Pe9805 **#5 Peter Pan Activity Tool** - brown knifelike tool with green crocodile and
purple tool with red tool attached. $2.00-2.50

❏ ❏   Pe9806 **#6 Tinker Bell Lantern** - Tinker Bell is inside small red lantern. $2.00-2.50

❏ ❏   Pe9807 **#7 Smee Light** - man in brown barrel with red flashlight effect. $2.50-3.50

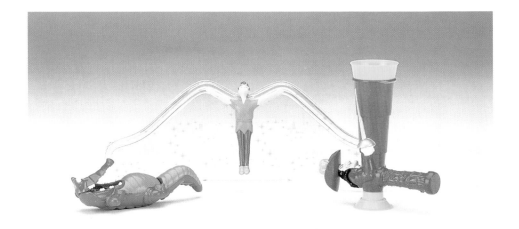

Pe9801-03

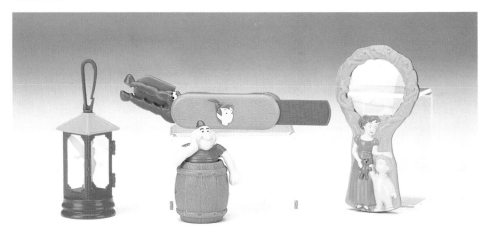

Pe9804-07

RECESS HAPPY MEAL, 1998

❏ ❏ Re9801 **#1 TJ** - boy with yellow hockey stick and red ball. 2 pieces. $1.50-2.00
❏ ❏ Re9802 **#2 Spinelli** - girl with green bat and white ball. 2 pieces. $1.50-2.00
❏ ❏ Re9803 **#3 Vince** - African-American boy with #1 on shirt and orange basketball. 2 pieces. $1.50-2.00
❏ ❏ Re9804 **#4 Gretchen** - girl with glasses and tennis racket and green ball. 2 pieces. $1.50-2.00
❏ ❏ Re9805 **#5 School Teacher Miss Finster** - teacher in yellow dress and purple ball. 2 pieces. $1.50-2.00
❏ ❏ Re9806 **#6 Gus** - boy with glasses and gold club and yellow ball. 2 pieces. $1.50-2.00
❏ ❏ Re9807 **#7 Mikey** - boy with white shirt and green ball. 2 pieces. $1.50-2.00

Re9801-04

Re9805-07

Simba's Pride Lion King Happy Meal, 1998

❏ ❏ Si9801 **#1 Kovu** - brown and black with yellow and orange eyes. $1.50-2.00
❏ ❏ Si9802 **#2 Zazu** -bird-like animal in blue, white, and orange. $1.50-2.00
❏ ❏ Si9803 **#3 Timon** - tan and brown animal. $1.50-2.00
❏ ❏ Si9804 **#4 Kiara** - tan with purple nose animal. $1.50-2.00
❏ ❏ Si9805 **#5 Pumbaa** - lion with tan and pink nose. $1.50-2.00
❏ ❏ Si9806 **#6 Ziro** - brown, black, and tan animal with a long nose. $1.50-2.00
❏ ❏ Si9807 **#7 Rafiki** - purple and white with a white beard. $1.50-2.00
❏ ❏ Si9808 **#8 Simba** - tan and brown fringe hair with a beard. $1.50-2.00

Si9801-04

Si9805-08

Tamagotchi Happy Meal, 1998

❏ ❏   To9801 **#1 Yellow Egg Shaped Tamagotchi.** $1.50-2.00

❏ ❏   To9802 **#2 Purple Egg Shaped with Green Dog Figure Tamagotchi.** 2 pieces.
                                                                   $1.50-2.00

❏ ❏   To9803 **#3 Green Egg Shaped Tamagotchi.** $1.50-2.00

❏ ❏   To9804 **#4 Red Egg Shaped Tamagotchi.** $1.50-2.00

❏ ❏   To9805 **#5 Blue Egg Shaped with Yellow Figure Tamagotchi.** 2 pieces. $1.50-2.00

❏ ❏   To9806 **#6 White Egg Shaped with Black and Red Figure Tamagotchi.** 2 pieces.
                                                                   $1.50-2.00

❏ ❏   To9807 **#7 Orange Egg Shaped Tamagotchi.** $1.50-2.00

❏ ❏   To9808 **#8 Blue Egg Shaped Tamagotchi.** $1.50-2.00

To9801-04

To9805-08

TEENIE BEANIE BABIES HAPPY MEAL, 1998

❏ ❏	Ty9801 **#1 Doby the Doberman** - brown and black.	$3.00-4.00
❏ ❏	Ty9802 **#2 Bongo the Monkey** - brown.	$3.00-4.00
❏ ❏	Ty9803 **#3 Twigs the Giraffe** - orange and yellow.	$3.00-4.00
❏ ❏	Ty9804 **#4 Inch the Worm** - yellow, orange, green, black, and purple.	$2.50-3.50
❏ ❏	Ty9805 **#5 Pincher the Lobster** - red.	$2.50-3.50
❏ ❏	Ty9806 **#6 Happy the Hippo** - purple.	$2.50-3.50
❏ ❏	Ty9807 **#7 Mel the Koala** - gray and white.	$2.50-3.50
❏ ❏	Ty9808 **#8 Scoop the Pelican** - large orange peak.	$2.50-3.50
❏ ❏	Ty9809 **#9 Bones the Dog** - tan with brown ears.	$2.50-3.50
❏ ❏	Ty9810 **#10 Zip the Cat** - black with white paws.	$2.50-3.50
❏ ❏	Ty9811 **#11 Waddle the Penguin** - black and white with orange feet.	$2.50-3.50
❏ ❏	Ty9812 **#12 Peanut the Elephant** - blue.	$2.50-3.50

Ty9801-04

110

Ty9805-08

Ty9809-12

1999

Furby Happy Meal, 1999

Style 1: Pushing tail makes Furby growl and moves eyes

❑ ❑	Fr9901 #1 **Black with pink tuft and belly.**		$4.00-5.00
❑ ❑	Fr9902 #2 **Black with white tuft and belly.**		$4.00-5.00
❑ ❑	Fr9903 #3 **Blue with pink tuft and belly.**		$4.00-5.00
❑ ❑	Fr9904 #4 **Blue with white tuft and belly.**		$4.00-5.00

Fr9901-02

Fr9903-04

❑	❑	Fr9905 **#5 Light green with pink tuft and belly.**	$4.00-5.00
❑	❑	Fr9906 **#6 Light green with white tuft and belly.**	$4.00-5.00
❑	❑	Fr9907 **#7 Purple with pink tuft and belly.**	$4.00-5.00
❑	❑	Fr9908 **#8 Purple with white tuft and belly.**	$4.00-5.00

Fr9905-06

Fr9907-08

❑	❑	Fr9909 **#9** Turquoise with pink tuft and belly.	$4.00-5.00
❑	❑	Fr9910 **#10** Turquoise with white tuft and belly.	$4.00-5.00

STYLE 2: PUSHING FORWARD MAKES FEET AND EARS MOVE

❑	❑	Fr9911 **#11** Blue with white tuft and belly.	$4.00-5.00
❑	❑	Fr9912 **#12** Blue with yellow tuft and white belly.	$4.00-5.00

Fr9909-10

Fr9911-12

❑	❑	Fr9913 **#13 Gray with white tuft and belly.**	$4.00-5.00
❑	❑	Fr9914 **#14 Gray with yellow tuft and white belly.**	$4.00-5.00
❑	❑	Fr9915 **#15 Green with white tuft and belly.**	$4.00-5.00
❑	❑	Fr9916 **#16 Green with yellow tuft and white belly.**	$4.00-5.00

Fr9913-14

Fr9915-16

❑	❑	Fr9917 **#17** Orange with white tuft and belly.	$4.00-5.00
❑	❑	Fr9918 **#18** Orange with yellow tuft and white belly.	$4.00-5.00
❑	❑	Fr9919 **#19** Purple with white tuft and belly.	$4.00-5.00
❑	❑	Fr9920 **#20** Purple with yellow tuft and white belly.	$4.00-5.00

Fr9917-18

Fr9919-20

116

❏ ❏	Fr9921 **#21 Light blue with green tuft.**		$4.00-5.00
❏ ❏	Fr9922 **#22 Light blue with purple tuft.**		$4.00-5.00
❏ ❏	Fr9923 **#23 Orange with green tuft.**		$4.00-5.00
❏ ❏	Fr9924 **#24 Orange with purple tuft.**		$4.00-5.00

Fr9921-22

Fr9923-24

❏ ❏ Fr9925 **#25 Pink with green tuft.** $4.00-5.00
❏ ❏ Fr9926 **#26 Pink with purple tuft.** $4.00-5.00
❏ ❏ Fr9927 **#27 Rust with green tuft.** $4.00-5.00
❏ ❏ Fr9928 **#28 Rust with purple tuft.** $4.00-5.00

Fr9925-26

Fr9927-28

❑	❑	Fr9929 **#29 Yellow with green tuft.**	$4.00-5.00
❑	❑	Fr9930 **#30 Yellow with purple tuft.**	$4.00-5.00

STYLE 4: PRESS FEET MAKES BEAK, EARS, AND EYES MOVE

❑	❑	Fr9931 **#31 Beige with dots and white tuft and belly.**	$4.00-5.00
❑	❑	Fr9932 **#32 Beige, no dots, with red tuft and white belly.**	$4.00-5.00

Fr9929-30

Fr9931-32

119

☐	☐	Fr9933 **#33 Gray with dots and white tuft and belly.**	$4.00-5.00
☐	☐	Fr9934 **#34 Gray, no dots, with red tuft and white belly.**	$4.00-5.00
☐	☐	Fr9935 **#35 Orange with dots and white tuft and belly.**	$4.00-5.00
☐	☐	Fr9936 **#36 Orange, no dots, with red tuft and white belly.**	$4.00-5.00

Fr9933-34

Fr9935-36

❏	❏	Fr9937 **#37 Purple with dots and white tuft and belly.**	$4.00-5.00
❏	❏	Fr9938 **#38 Purple, no dots, and red tuft and white belly.**	$4.00-5.00
❏	❏	Fr9939 **#39 Yellow with dots and white tuft and belly.**	$4.00-5.00
❏	❏	Fr9940 **#40 Yellow, no dots, and red tuft and white belly.**	$4.00-5.00

Fr9937-38

Fr9939-40

Style 5: Furby says, "Eek!" when turned upside down

❑ ❑	Fr9941 **#41 Blue with white tuft.**	$4.00-5.00
❑ ❑	Fr9942 **#42 Blue with yellow tuft.**	$4.00-5.00
❑ ❑	Fr9943 **#43 Light green with white tuft.**	$4.00-5.00
❑ ❑	Fr9944 **#44 Light green with yellow tuft.**	$4.00-5.00

Fr9941-42

Fr9943-44

❑ ❑ Fr9945 **#45 Purple with white tuft.** $4.00-5.00
❑ ❑ Fr9946 **#46 Purple with yellow tuft.** $4.00-5.00
❑ ❑ Fr9947 **#47 Red with white tuft.** $4.00-5.00
❑ ❑ Fr9948 **#48 Red with yellow tuft.** $4.00-5.00

Fr9945-46

Fr9947-48

| | | Fr9949 #49 White with white tuft. | $4.00-5.00 |
| | | Fr9950 #50 White with yellow tuft. | $4.00-5.00 |

STYLE 6: FURBY PLAYS "PEEKABOO" WITH EARS WHEN TAIL IS PRESSED

| | | Fr9951 #51 Black with black tuft. | $4.00-5.00 |
| | | Fr9952 #52 Black with purple tuft. | $4.00-5.00 |

Fr9949-50

Fr9951-52

124

		Fr9953 **#53 Blue with black tuft.**	$4.00-5.00
		Fr9954 **#54 Blue with purple tuft.**	$4.00-5.00
		Fr9955 **#55 Light green with black tuft.**	$4.00-5.00
		Fr9956 **#56 Light green with purple tuft.**	$4.00-5.00

Fr9953-54

Fr9955-56

125

❑ ❑	Fr9957 **#57** Orange with black tuft.	$4.00-5.00
❑ ❑	Fr9958 **#58** Orange with purple tuft.	$4.00-5.00
❑ ❑	Fr9959 **#59** Teal with black tuft.	$4.00-5.00
❑ ❑	Fr9960 **#60** Teal with purple tuft.	$4.00-5.00

Fr9957-58

Fr9959-60

STYLE 7: PUSHING TAIL MAKES FURBY SQUEAK AND MOVES EYELIDS AND BEAK

❏ ❏	Fr9961 **#61 Gray with black tuft and belly.**		$4.00-5.00
❏ ❏	Fr9962 **#62 Gray with white tuft and belly.**		$4.00-5.00
❏ ❏	Fr9963 **#63 Green with black tuft and belly.**		$4.00-5.00
❏ ❏	Fr9964 **#64 Green with white tuft and belly.**		$4.00-5.00

Fr9961-62

Fr9963-64

127

☐ ☐	Fr9965 **#65 Purple with black tuft and belly.**	$4.00-5.00
☐ ☐	Fr9966 **#66 Purple with white tuft and belly.**	$4.00-5.00
☐ ☐	Fr9967 **#67 Red with black tuft and belly.**	$4.00-5.00
☐ ☐	Fr9968 **#68 Red with white tuft and belly.**	$4.00-5.00

Fr9965-66

Fr9967-68

| | Fr9969 **#69** Yellow with black tuft and belly. | $4.00-5.00 |
| | Fr9970 **#70** Yellow with white tuft and belly. | $4.00-5.00 |

STYLE 8: ROLLING BALL ON BACK MOVES THE EYES AND EARS
| | Fr9971 **#71** Black with blue tuft and red belly. | $4.00-5.00 |
| | Fr9972 **#72** Black with pink tuft and belly. | $4.00-5.00 |

Fr9969-70

Fr9971-72

❏	❏	Fr9973 **#73** Dark blue with blue tuft and red belly.	$4.00-5.00
❏	❏	Fr9974 **#74** Dark blue with pink tuft and belly.	$4.00-5.00
❏	❏	Fr9975 **#75** Light blue with blue tuft and red belly.	$4.00-5.00
❏	❏	Fr9976 **#76** Light blue with pink tuft and belly.	$4.00-5.00

Fr9973-74

Fr9975-76

❏	❏	Fr9977 **#77 Gray with blue tuft and red belly.**	$4.00-5.00
❏	❏	Fr9978 **#78 Gray with spots and pink tuft and belly.**	$4.00-5.00
❏	❏	Fr9979 **#79 Pink with blue tuft and red belly.**	$4.00-5.00
❏	❏	Fr9980 **#80 Pink with pink tuft and belly.**	$4.00-5.00

Fr9977-78

Fr9979-80

MULAN HAPPY MEAL, 1999

❏	❏	Mu9901 **Ling** - on red base spinner.	$1.50-2.00
❏	❏	Mu9902 **Mulan & Cri-Kee** - wearing a green shirt holding Cri-Kee on her back. 2 pieces	
		launcher.	$1.50-2.00
❏	❏	Mu9903 **Khan** - wearing a black cape spinner.	$1.50-2.00
❏	❏	Mu9904 **Mushu** - gray statue with red figure on disc. 2 pieces launcher.	$1.50-2.00
❏	❏	Mu9905 **Yao** - wearing red trim spinner.	$1.50-2.00
❏	❏	Mu9906 **Shang** - wearing green trim. 2 pieces launcher.	$1.50-2.00
❏	❏	Mu9907 **Chien Po** - wearing gray with blue trim spinner.	$1.50-2.00
❏	❏	Mu9908 **Shan Yu** - wearing blue with brown bird. 2 pieces launcher.	$1.50-2.00

Mu9901-04

Mu9905-08

WINNIE THE POOH HAPPY MEAL, 1999

❏ ❏	Wi9901	**Winnie the Pooh clip-on plush head.**	$2.50-4.00
❏ ❏	Wi9902	**Rabbit clip-on plush head.**	$2.50-4.00
❏ ❏	Wi9903	**Tigger clip-on plush head.**	$2.50-4.00
❏ ❏	Wi9904	**Gopher clip-on plush head.**	$2.50-4.00
❏ ❏	Wi9905	**Piglet clip-on plush head.**	$2.50-4.00
❏ ❏	Wi9906	**Roo clip-on plush head.**	$2.50-4.00
❏ ❏	Wi9907	**Eeyore clip-on plush head.**	$2.50-4.00
❏ ❏	Wi9908	**Owl clip-on plush head.**	$2.50-4.00

Wi9901-08

McDonald's Happy Meal Toys from Around the World

McDonald's gives out different Happy Meal toys in restaurants outside the United States. If you have parents, relatives, or friends that travel, ask them to please bring back some toys from their trip. When you travel, you can collect toys from the different McDonald's restaurants around the world. The toys from different countries are different from the toys at your neighborhood McDonald's. Remember, McDonald's is located in over 114 different countries all around the world! The United States is one country and Germany is another country. How many different countries can you name in your collection? Can you name all 114 different countries? The challenge is "to have the most FUN collecting McDonald's Happy Meal toys" and "to collect as many McDonald's Happy Meal toys from as MANY different countries as possible.

Here are some special international toy sets from all over the globe. Remember, the one with the most toys from the many different countries wins! So, get to it, and HAVE FUN COLLECTING!

1990

CANADA

CANADA McDONALDLAND FIGURINES PROMOTION, 1990

❑	❑	Can Fi9001 **#1 Figurine Birdie** - yellow with maple leaf under arches.	$5.00-10.00
❑	❑	Can Fi9002 **#2 Figurine Hamburglar** - white with arms down to side.	$5.00-10.00
❑	❑	Can Fi9003 **#3 Figurine Grimace** - purple with baseball cap turned to side.	$5.00-10.00
❑	❑	Can Fi9004 **#4 Figurine Ronald** - red with arms outstretched.	$20.00-25.00

Can Fi9001-04

1991

ENGLAND

ENGLAND CONNECT-A-CARS HAPPY MEAL, 1991

☐ ☐   Uk Co9101 **#1 Birdie Sports Coupe** - waving in pink car. 2 pieces. $4.00-5.00
☐ ☐   Uk Co9102 **#2 Grimace Speedster** - waving in white car. 2 pieces. $4.00-5.00
☐ ☐   Uk Co9103 **#3 Hamburglar Cabriolet** - waving in yellow car. 2 pieces. $4.00-5.00
☐ ☐   Uk Co9104 **#4 Ronald Roadster** - waving in red car. 2 pieces. $4.00-5.00

Uk Co9101-04

1992

ENGLAND

ENGLAND SPORTS BUDDIES HAPPY MEAL, 1992

☐ ☐ Uk Bu9201 **#1 Hammer Thrower** - black hair with yellow rope and green headband. 3 pieces. $5.00-8.00

☐ ☐ Uk Bu9202 **#2 Javelin Thrower** - brown hair and blue shoes and orange headband and pink shorts. 3 pieces. $5.00-8.00

☐ ☐ Uk Bu9203 **#3 Track Relay Runner** - red hair and pink shorts and white shoes. 3 pieces. $5.00-8.00

☐ ☐ Uk Bu9204 **#4 Weight Lifter** - yellow hair with blue weights wearing pink, magenta belt. 3 pieces. $5.00-8.00

Uk Bu9201-04

HOLLAND

HOLLAND DRAGONETTES HAPPY MEAL, 1992

☐ ☐ Hol Dr9201 **#1 Gigi - Purple Dragon with Black and White Baton.** $5.00-8.00
☐ ☐ Hol Dr9202 **#2 Lucky - Yellow Dragon with Red Books.** $5.00-8.00
☐ ☐ Hol Dr9203 **#3 Puff - Green Dragon with Red Bottle.** $5.00-8.00
☐ ☐ Hol Dr9204 **#4 Ritchi - Blue Dragon with Red Ball with Foot Peg.** $5.00-8.00

Hol Dr9201-04

JAPAN

JAPAN DRAGONETTES HAPPY MEAL, 1992

☐ ☐ Jpn Dr9301 **#1 Gigi** - purple dragon with yellow candle. $5.00-8.00
☐ ☐ Jpn Dr9302 **#2 Lucky** - yellow dragon with red French Fries container. $5.00-8.00
☐ ☐ Jpn Dr9303 **#3 Puff** - green dragon with red container. $5.00-8.00
☐ ☐ Jpn Dr9304 **#4 Ritchie** - blue dragon with red ball and no double foot peg. $5.00-8.00

Jpn Dr9301-04

1993

ENGLAND

ENGLAND BARBIE HAPPY MEAL, 1993

- ☐ ☐ Uk Ba9301 **#1 Barbie Crystal Heart** - yellow hair with purple and white dress with hearts. $2.00-4.00
- ☐ ☐ Uk Ba9302 **#2 Barbie Hollywood Hair Barbie** - gold short dress and pink star base. $2.00-4.00
- ☐ ☐ Uk Ba9303 **#3 Barbie My First Ballerina** - purple ballerina dress with brown long hair. $2.00-4.00
- ☐ ☐ Uk Ba9304 **#4 Barbie Sea Holiday** - blonde hair and dark blue cloth dress. $3.00-5.00

Uk Ba9301-04

GERMANY

GERMANY ROCK 'N ROLL BAND MCTWIST HAPPY MEAL, 1993

- ☐ ☐ Ger Hm9301 **#1 Birdie with Mike.** $3.00-4.00
- ☐ ☐ Ger Hm9302 **#2 Grimace with Saxophone.** $3.00-4.00
- ☐ ☐ Ger Hm9303 **#3 Hamburglar with Drums.** $3.00-4.00
- ☐ ☐ Ger Hm9304 **#4 Ronald with Guitar.** $3.00-4.00

Ger Hm9301-04

GERMANY SNOW DOMES HAPPY MEAL, 1993

❏ ❏   Ger Sn9301 **#1 Snow Dome Ronald on Ice Skates.** $5.00-7.00
❏ ❏   Ger Sn9302 **#2 Snow Dome Snowman in front of McDonald's.** $5.00-7.00
❏ ❏   Ger Sn9303 **#3 Snow Dome Ronald as Snowman.** $5.00-7.00

Ger Sn9301-03

DENMARK

DENMARK ALADDIN HAPPY MEAL, 1993

❏ ❏   Den Al9301 **#1 Aladdin & Jasmine** - on magic rug. $3.00-4.00
❏ ❏   Den Al9302 **#2 Genie** - in magic bottle. $3.00-4.00
❏ ❏   Den Al9303 **#3 Jafar** - black cape standing. $3.00-4.00
❏ ❏   Den Al9304 **#4 Sultan** - sitting folded arms. $3.00-4.00

Den Al9301-04

NEW ZEALAND ALADDIN HAPPY MEAL, 1993

❏ ❏ Zea Al9301 **#1 Aladdin** - in Abu Monkey vehicle. $4.00-5.00
❏ ❏ Zea Al9302 **#2 Jafar** - in the Lago Bird vehicle. $4.00-5.00
❏ ❏ Zea Al9303 **#3 Jasmine** - in the Rajah Tiger vehicle. $4.00-5.00
❏ ❏ Zea Al9304 **#4 Genie** - in the Lamp vehicle. $4.00-5.00

Zea Al9301-04

NEW ZEALAND BIG BUDDIES HAPPY MEAL, 1993

❏ ❏ Zea Bu9301 **#1 Figurine Birdie** - large 3 1/2" figurine. $7.00-10.00
❏ ❏ Zea Bu9302 **#2 Figurine Grimace** - large 4" figurine. $7.00-10.00
❏ ❏ Zea Bu9303 **#3 Figurine Hamburglar** - large 3 3/4" figurine. $7.00-10.00
❏ ❏ Zea Bu9304 **#4 Figurine Ronald** - large 5" figurine. $7.00-10.00

Zea Bu9303

Zea Bu9301

Zea Bu9302

Zea Bu9304

JAPAN

JAPAN SNOOPY WORLD TOUR HAPPY MEAL, 1999

SNOOPY WORLD TOUR FIGURES:

❏ ❏   Jpn Sn9901 **#1 Snoopy in Taiwan** - red jacket. $6.00-8.00
❏ ❏   Jpn Sn9902 **#2 Snoopy in Scotland** - gray hat and shirt. $6.00-8.00
❏ ❏   Jpn Sn9903 **#3 Snoopy in the Wild West** - red cowboy hat. $6.00-8.00
❏ ❏   Jpn Sn9904 **#4 Snoopy in Malaysia** - green shirt with flower. $6.00-8.00

Jpn Sn9901-04

❏ ❏   Jpn Sn9905 **#5 Snoopy in Germany** - blue hat. $6.00-8.00
❏ ❏   Jpn Sn9906 **#6 Snoopy in the U.S.A.** - red, white, and blue hat. $6.00-8.00
❏ ❏   Jpn Sn9907 **#7 Snoopy in the United Kingdom** - black hat. $6.00-8.00
❏ ❏   Jpn Sn9908 **#8 Snoopy in China** - red suit and black hat. $6.00-8.00

Jpn Sn9905-08

❑	❑	Jpn Sn9909 **#9 Snoopy in Indonesia** - red hat with racket.	$6.00-8.00
❑	❑	Jpn Sn9910 **#10 Snoopy in Switzerland** - black, yellow, and white vest.	$6.00-8.00
❑	❑	Jpn Sn9911 **#11 Snoopy in Singapore** - blue shirt.	$6.00-8.00
❑	❑	Jpn Sn9912 **#12 Snoopy in the Japan** - black shirt.	$6.00-8.00

Jpn Sn9909-12

❑	❑	Jpn Sn9913 **#13 Snoopy in the Philippines** - red and yellow hat and shirt.	$6.00-8.00
❑	❑	Jpn Sn9914 **#14 Snoopy in Italy** - blue and red hat and shirt. 2 pieces.	$6.00-8.00
❑	❑	Jpn Sn9915 **#15 Snoopy in Latin America** - blue and yellow shirt.	$6.00-8.00
❑	❑	Jpn Sn9916 **#16 Snoopy in the Alaska** - green hat and coat.	$6.00-8.00

Jpn Sn9913-16

❑	❑	Jpn Sn9917 **#17 Snoopy in France** - lavender shirt.	$6.00-8.00
❑	❑	Jpn Sn9918 **#18 Snoopy in Australia** - brown and yellow hat.	$6.00-8.00
❑	❑	Jpn Sn9919 **#19 Snoopy in Korea** - blue and red hat.	$6.00-8.00
❑	❑	Jpn Sn9920 **#20 Snoopy in the Mexico** - blue, red, green, and yellow hat. 2 pieces.	$6.00-8.00

Jpn Sn9917-20

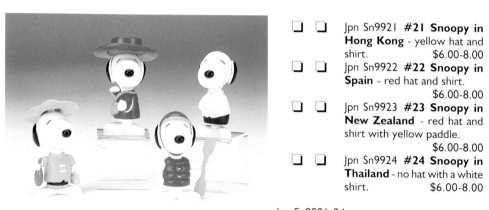

❑ ❑	Jpn Sn9921 **#21 Snoopy in Hong Kong** - yellow hat and shirt.	$6.00-8.00
❑ ❑	Jpn Sn9922 **#22 Snoopy in Spain** - red hat and shirt.	$6.00-8.00
❑ ❑	Jpn Sn9923 **#23 Snoopy in New Zealand** - red hat and shirt with yellow paddle.	$6.00-8.00
❑ ❑	Jpn Sn9924 **#24 Snoopy in Thailand** - no hat with a white shirt.	$6.00-8.00

Jpn Sn9921-24

❑	❑	Jpn Sn9925 **#25 Snoopy in Norway** - yellow horns on hat.	$6.00-8.00
❑	❑	Jpn Sn9926 **#26 Snoopy in Canada** - brown and red hat. 2 pieces.	$6.00-8.00
❑	❑	Jpn Sn9927 **#27 Snoopy in Hawaii** - purple sunglasses and shirt.	$6.00-8.00
❑	❑	Jpn Sn9928 **#28 Snoopy in Mongolia** - brown and white hat.	$6.00-8.00

Jpn Sn9925-28

INDEX